Letters from Vietnam
A Daughter's Search For Her Father

Letters from Vietnam
A Daughter's Search For Her Father

Jacqueline Lundquist
and
Lt. Col. Donald C. Lundquist

H
HAR-ANAND
PUBLICATIONS PVT LTD

For
Mom and Dad

Copyright © 2011 Jacqueline Lundquist and Lt. Col. Donald C. Lundquist

First Published: 2011

Published by Ashok Gosain and Ashish Gosain for:
HAR-ANAND PUBLICATIONS PVT LTD
E-49/3, Okhla Industrial Area, Phase-II, New Delhi-110020
Tel.: 41603490 Fax: 011-41708607
E-mail: info@haranandpublications.com
Website: www.haranandpublications.com

Printed in India at Vinayak Offset

Foreword

I remember the first time I heard Natalie Cole sing 'Unforgettable' with her father, Nat King Cole. I thought the song was one of the most beautiful collaborations between daughter and father that I had ever heard. Of course, they never did record that song together, but through the miracle of modern technology they released an album of duets long after his death. I feel that this endeavor is similar.

This story takes place over the span of 42 years and in four very distinct periods of time. I suppose all good stories take years to develop and I feel that this couldn't have been written or assembled a moment sooner than it has.

My father's journey was finite and mandated by the US Army. My journey has taken longer and it is fate that has dictated its path.

My dad began to write these letters in the summer of 1967 on his way to Vietnam. I read them in the summer of 1997 in Cleveland. I assembled the book in the summer of 2000 while living in India. My publisher said he would only publish this work after I made my own journey to Vietnam. That took another 9 years to complete. Only when the circumstances of my life drove me to seek out my father, could I call up the courage to move forward on this project.

I am grateful to my family and the many friends that encouraged me on my journey. You were with me every step of the way. I am especially thankful to my steadfast friend, Indriena Basarah, who made the journey to Vietnam with me. Her beloved father passed away soon after we returned from Vietnam and I believe the love she had for her father was instrumental in helping me find mine.

Introduction

I got to know my father in the summer of 1997, when I was 7 months pregnant with my son, Sam. I was 34. It was 28 years after he died.

I had always known it existed. My mother had told me when I was old enough to understand. She had taken it with her the many times we had moved and always put it on the top shelf of her closet. She'd remind me from time to time. When I got married and moved away, I took it with me and put it on the top shelf of my closet. It wasn't that I lacked interest, for I was always asking my father's Army buddies about him. Often, the older I got, I would find my mother or my father's friends staring at me in a peculiar manner as if they had seen a ghost. I looked just like him ... he would have said that too ... he would have been so proud today. Quite simply, I just lacked the courage to open it, for by doing so, I would need to confront a loss that I had managed to bury deep inside for all those years.

It was a box filled with almost 300 hundred letters my father had written to my mother and me the year he was in Vietnam. It contained over 20 hours of tapes he recorded in his hooch in Chu Lai as the Vietnam War raged around him. It also contained the many hours of tapes that I, as a three year old, and my mother and grandmother recorded to divert my father's attention, if briefly, from the loneliness, sadness and savageness of war.

Perhaps it was the prospect of becoming a parent and trying to understand the implications that made me curious. Perhaps it was because I was in a loving and secure relationship with a man that gave me courage. Perhaps my hormones were to blame and I was looking for a "real" reason to cry. Whatever the impetus, I sat down that beautiful Cleveland summer weekend and read and listened and wept and got to know a most remarkable husband, father, soldier and man.

My parents met in the town of Fulda, Germany. My father was a young American officer and my mother a striking, tall German blond. It was love at first sight, for my father, at least. He was seated at the bar of the Hotel Lenz with another soldier and my mother entered with two friends. My father took one look and told his buddy, "That's the girl I'm going to marry." Having spent her youth running from bombs and holed up in a bunker in World War II courtesy of the United States, her ideal man was not this American soldier who had invited her for a dance. She declined his offer and promptly left.

My father, as the story goes, spent the next several weeks driving up and down the streets of Fulda searching for her in vain. He did, however, find the friends she had come with that first evening in the hotel and befriended them. Hans Rolbetzky was a German doctor who was married to my mother's best friend, Ulli. His charm and charisma won the two over and they convinced my mother, Ruth Oestreich, to meet this wonderful young soldier, Lieutenant Donald Carl Lundquist. The rest, as they say, is history.

They married in Germany in 1959 and then moved to Ft. Knox, Kentucky where I was born in 1964. The next posting took them back to Wuerzburg, Germany. After two years, they were transferred to Ft. Hood, Texas where they lived until August of 1967 where this book begins.

My father went to Vietnam as a Major with the 1/1 Cavalry Squadron. He loved the military and he loved his job. He actually lied about his age and joined the Army when he was just 17 years old. He served in Korea where he was heavily decorated and then became a commissioned officer. He finally earned his college degree from the University of Omaha when he was 34 years old. He went to Vietnam when he was 36 to act as executive office of the 1st Squadron 1st Cavalry 1st Armored Division.

My parents decided that my mother and I would go back and live with my grandmother (Mutti) in Germany while my father was in Vietnam. It was a way for them to save some money and an opportunity for my mother to help take care of my grandmother who was sick with cancer. My mother's two sisters, Lilo and Ilse, and their husbands, Ernst and Werner, and my five cousins were all nearby.

I am now exactly the age my mother was when her husband went off to fight a war she didn't quite understand. My son is the same age I was when my father left me for reasons I certainly didn't understand.

These are his letters. This is his story.

DEPARTMENT OF THE ARMY
HEADQUARTERS, 1ST ARMORED DIVISION (OLD IRONSIDES)
Fort Hood, Texas 76545

AKDFA-GA   12 February 1967

Major Donald C. Lundquist, 097939, Armor
Hq, 3d Infantry Division
APO New York 09036

Dear Major Lundquist:

DA assignment instructions have been received allocating
you to the 1st Squadron, 1st Cavalry (First U. S. Dragoons),
1st Armored Division. You are presently programmed to serve
as squadron executive officer.

The squadron commander is presently on TDY in the RVN, but
will return shortly before your arrival. The acting squadron
commander is Major Matt O. Delmas, Armor (nominally assigned
as assistant to the ACofS, G3.)

I am inclosing a recently issued Station Report, and
Division Officers Directory for your information.

We are looking forward to your joining us in the 1st Armored Division (Old Ironsides). If there is anything I can do
prior to your arrival, or information you desire, please write
me direct, or telephone upon your arrival in the CONUS. The
telephone number at Fort Hood is 6201 or 5528.

Again, welcome to Old Ironsides, and particularly to the
First Dragoons.

Sincerely,

EUGENE F. GANLEY
LTC, GS
ACofS, G1

Incls
2-a/s

4 August, 1967

Fort Hood Army Base, Killeen, Texas

Dearest Ruth and Jacqueline,

I am sitting here in the empty kitchen writing letters to everyone and it is very quiet.

I know that yesterday was very sad and emotional for all of us. I felt so empty and helpless to say something to cheer you up and make you relax for the love and respect I have for you and Jacqueline. Know and feel, honey that the year will fly by quickly and we shall all be together again - happy and together again.

It was so hot and I was so upset, I drove back to Killeen shortly after your plane took off. I stopped at the club to eat and joined Col. and Mrs. Taylor the division Chief of Staff for dinner. It is his last day as he is leaving for Vietnam, too.

This morning at 11:15am your telegram arrived. I'm happy you arrived well. Please tell Mutti, Werner and Ilse, Ernst and Lilo and all the children and friends to take care of you both, give them my love and best regards.

I learned from Butch today that the whole squadron is flying to California instead of going by train. I fly from Killeen Base Airport at 2:30 p.m. 9 August and arrive in California at 6:33 p.m. and load on the ship to depart around 2:00 p.m. on the 10th. Approximately 30-31 August we arrive in Vung Jau, the port city southwest of Saigon.

You realize I can't mail letters at sea, but I shall write you several times before I leave here, in California and at sea.

Be brave, be patient, be understanding, and this year will pass quickly, darling.

Remember that I love you both so, so, dearly. You both are all that I have so don't worry for me. I shall always take care and remember you are there waiting.

A special hug and kiss for Jacqueline from her Daddy.

I love you, Ruth.

Always,

Your Don

7 August '67
Monday Afternoon

Dear Ruth and Jacqueline,

I was hoping to hear from you before I left and your welcome letter arrived this afternoon. Sorry to hear Stinky got sick and I hope by now she is well and that you both are rested.

I'm at work trying to get 10,000 and one last minute details taken care of - baggage and all kinds of little things. I'm all packed now and just have to wait to leave.

I still leave on Wednesday from here and Thursday afternoon from California.

On the map I gave you you'll see North of Chu Lai is a city called Da Nang. That is where we will land and I presume stay for a while.

Darling, do me a big favor! In your letters don't mention the time. Time will go quickly if you keep busy, do things and are a brave girl. I'm not going over there with any wild ideas about becoming a hero and winning medals and things. I just will do my job safely and always before me is the mental picture of you and Stinky both in my head and heart. Next year I'll be back safe and sound and a bit skinny, but we shall all be together again.

O.K.? So - no more talk of time or being safe, etc. I will. And you do your very best to keep busy, do things, work, help Mutti and don't think so much.

Tell Mutti that I said for her to stay well and let Jacqueline cure her ills with her love and sunshine. God is with her and Donald Carl sends his love.

Tomorrow, they have a little ceremony on the parade field as a goodbye gesture at 4:00pm when the temperature is around 101 degrees. Whew! It sure will be hot.

Col. H just returned from leave, came in for a few minutes and took off again for home. Oh well, guess there is nothing for him to really do now.

```
MRS. D.C LUNDQUIST
14TH CAV. REGT.
APO # 09036, N.Y. N.Y

                                        8¢
                                      AIRMAIL
                                       STAMP

"AIRMAIL"      MAJ. D.C. LUNDQUIST
               HQ'S 1/1 CAV. SQDN.
               APO #96374 SAN FRANCISCO,
                          CALIFORNIA
```

NEW
← ADDRESS
WRITE NOW
& LETTERS WILL
BE WAITING
FOR ME WHEN
I ARRIVE.

Please say hello to everyone for me, honey, and God bless you and Jacqueline, strong, be brave, be busy and before you know it we will all be singing in the sunshine of laughter and happiness in school or some other assignment.

I love you both so, so dearly.

Kisses to Jacqueline.

Always,

Your Don and Daddy

Monday, 15 August '67
Pacific Ocean

My Dearest Ruth and Jacqueline,

Daddy is now at sea almost six days and the Pacific Ocean is calm, cool and so far it has been a pleasant trip. I have a large stateroom with desk, private shower and chairs, etc. Quite comfortable.

It is the same thing every day. Get up at 7:00. Eat, read, eat, read, inspect, walk around, eat, sleep. Not really too much else to do. My soldiers and officers are doing well. For many of them it is their first time at sea. They seem to have their sea legs by now.

Food is absolutely delicious and we have far too many choices at every meal. I have had to cut down because it's too much. On or about the 17 or 18 of August we will stop on the Island of Okinawa in the Sea of Japan for more supplies and get a one-day pause or rest on land. Then we should be off again and on to Da Nang, Vietnam.

When we arrived in San Francisco by airplane it was 70 degrees, so cool, that it was like our apartment in Killeen when it was real cool. A pleasant change of pace to the 101 degrees when we left.

In a few days, it will get very hot in the South Pacific so my next few lines will be warm ones, I'm sure.

Till a bit later, sweeties. Daddy sends his love and hugs and kisses.

Here it is 23 August! The ship had turned south for two days to avoid a typhoon/hurricane and we are now 1½ days from Okinawa. It appears we will have a one-day rest and perhaps we can all get off and do some sightseeing and sleep cool one night.

I have been reading one or two pocket size books per day and eating too much and because of the heat I'm just dripping wet all the time.

Also, been playing poker for 25 and 50 cent limits and have made a few dollars. Enough so I bought a small pair of binoculars Japanese model for $17.50 and a cheap GE pocket sized transistor radio.

This morning I have been washing all my socks and underclothes just to keep busy. Depending on how long we have free in Okinawa, I will try to send Jacqueline a little gift or toy.

For this day I'll say again I love you both.

Today, 25th August, the most interesting event was watching the flying fish. Little ones about six inches long that pop out of the water and fly like a bird about 50 meters and then fall back into the sea.

Each day it becomes hotter and very sticky. Rather uncomfortable sleeping.

I shall end this letter now so in the morning when we dock in Okinawa it will be mailed promptly.

Soon as I get to Vietnam, I'll send you some more money. Use it slowly and carefully, honey.

Regards to all at home. Special love to you my Big Momma and to Daddy's little Jacqueline.

Love you both so dearly and miss you just as much.

Always.

Your Don and Big Daddy

Friday 25 August '67
Okinawa

Dearest Ruth and Jacqueline,

Just a few lines today. Our ship's visit in Okinawa was a short one. Enough for everyone to get off for a few hours, walk around, have an ice-cold beer, do a quick shopping tour and then back on board before dark.

Several of my officers and I got off the ship and donated one pint of our blood for our soldiers in Vietnam and then took a military sedan ride into the small city of Koza for lunch and bought some postcards.

I bought Stinky a doll in Japanese costume. One more to look at rather than to play with, and I got you a small gift. Couldn't mail them properly so I'll wait till we arrive in Vietnam.

Sunday, the ship's Captain is giving a dinner for all the officers. It should be pleasant as the food has been just great up to this time.

Soon we shall arrive and I am anxious to get settled, learn exactly where we will be and what our job is. Butch and the Colonel will probably greet us and then hard work will begin.

I hope it stays hard and keeps me busy so the time will fly very quickly.

I hope all is well with Mutti and that you and Jacqueline are more settled down and rested now. Have you looked for an apartment yet? How is everyone? Have you seen your friends? Keep busy, honey.

Love you, Want you, Need you both.

Love Always,

Your Don and Daddy

P.S. XXXX KISSES!

Sunday 27 August '67
At Sea

Dearest Ruth,

Good morning, Sweetie. I awoke very early this morning. It was cool for once and I couldn't sleep anymore.

For the last couple of days I was mentally preparing a list of things I wanted you to send me - little things that you can't get in Vietnam.

I went to the cabin next door which is the Chief's and was drinking coffee with him and told him about what I was going to write you for and he said, "Good gracious, Major, don't do that. I will give you all you want from the ship's store for free."

After breakfast, he had the storekeeper take me on a tour of the ship's storerooms ... food, meat, vegetables, just everything ... like a large warehouse for a supermarket ... and I picked out:

1   case of Instant Coffee
2   cases of Assorted Kool-Aid, enough to make 576 gallons
1   case of Pineapple Juice
1   case of Beef Bullion Cubes

So, I guess I saved $25 to $35. That was quite a friendly gesture, don't you think?

It is absolutely amazing how much food they can carry - enough for 5,000 men for six months at sea.

Today, Sunday the 27th, is our last day at sea, as tomorrow morning we arrive in Da Nang. Tonight the ship's Captain is giving a dinner with just everything one would want to eat. I shall enclose a menu to show how good we have eaten just about every day.

The trip has been restful, peaceful and so much routine that we will all be glad to get off and get busy.

I have taken very few pictures on board because of lack of interest. Some of the other rolls I will send off to be developed just as soon as I arrive and will send them to you, honey.

In a few minutes, we are going to take a tour of the bridge. That is where the Captain runs the ship - way up on top.

Kisses and my love to you and Jacqueline.

Love you both so.

Always,

Your Don and Daddy

29 August '67
Tuesday
9:00am

Dearest Ruth and Jacqueline,

I'm sitting in the Captain's quarters on a Navy LST en route from Da Nang south along the coast to Chu Lai, that's about 50 miles south of Da Nang. An LST looks like this

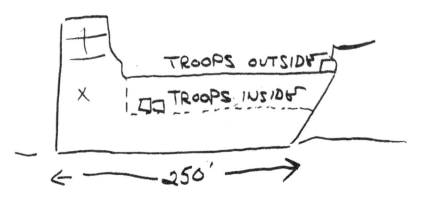

We arrived in Da Nang yesterday at about 6 a.m. Col. H came out to sea in a small launch and we have been talking business since. While the big ship was anchored in the harbor at sea, this LST pulled alongside and for almost 20 hours we moved ammunition, equipment and our men slowly onto this ship.

We are all aboard and now steaming south around 10 miles per hour in a calm sea and expect to land on the sandy beach of Chu Lai around 1:30 p.m. today.

I'll be glad to get on land and really get to work. Not for any reason other than it was rather dull and too routine aboard ship.

From the information Col. H has given me, our mission does not appear to be too difficult. So don't worry. I'm very anxious to see Butch and see what he has to say. All our tanks, vehicles and equipment are already here and on the sand dunes of the beach, waiting for us.

The men are all rested and eager to get to work.

The land here is very mountainous just a mile or so inland from the shore, very green, beautiful scenery, so far not too hot and rains, a short shower every hour or so.

Col. H didn't have any mail for me from you. Perhaps Butch does. I hope so. As I suggested before, I believe it would be faster service, cheaper too, for you to mail me letters from Downs Barracks in Fulda.

Had a king-sized breakfast a bit ago and a good fresh-water shower. I was up all night long supervising the loading of this ship so I shall try to get a few hours rest before we land later on.

Tonight, I'll wait to see if I have any mail from you and finish this letter later. I love you my Ruth and Stinky.

Chu Lai 2:30pm

The 1/1 Cavalry is here! The Colonel and I took a motor launch into the beach and we had a short proper ceremony as the troops unloaded. Major Dionne the short, fat, happy little major and the great big fat major who put on the skits in the officer's club in Wuerzburg were on hand to greet me here. Half the staff from the 3rd Infantry Division is here.

We will spend a few days directly on this sandy white beach and get organized. Butch has things under hand and all is well.

I've never seen so many Marines, ships, Navy jets, aircraft carriers, etc. Not too many Army men up here, just Marines. But that is changing quickly. After the National elections on 3 September, we will probably get busier and move again to a more permanent location.

All is well, darling. I'm here and work shall keep me very busy. I haven't had time this hectic day to find out too much but in the next days, I shall.

Kisses and hugs to my Jacqueline and my dearest love to you, my darling. Hello to Mutti.

Always.

Your Don and Daddy

30 August '67
6:15 p.m.

Dearest Ruth and Jacqueline,

Today has been a real busy day for our men! They are unloading and preparing all the tanks and vehicles. They are drawing their ammunition and checking everything, cleaning weapons.

All the men are about 1 mile from here on some sand dunes. Butch, Colonel and I are living temporarily with the 2/11 Cavalry Squadron Officers right on the beach on a hill. It's quite nice with a bed, refrigerator, fan, shower, etc.

Tomorrow, we move down the road about 8-10 miles north from here and will stay in this new area for a while. So far all is rather easy, quiet and routine.

Chu Lai is a tremendous U.S. Marine jet fighter base which bombs North Vietnam 24 hours a day. We and many other units are responsible for protecting the airbase from Vietcongs.

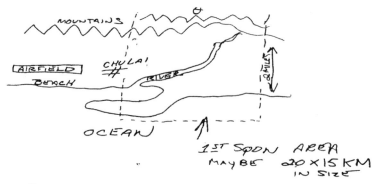

All is well, safe and so far easy. Don't worry, sweetie. I met our boss, a Brigadeer General who is a real soldier, down to earth and I like him. Good News.

I received your letter of 22 August and Jacqueline's drawing for Daddy. It is wonderful to hear from you and I understand every word so you just write half German/half English or any way but write often and a few lines, but write. I'm happy you were able to get a car. Just drive safely and slowly, honey.

Perhaps you will feel less nervous when a few weeks more go by and the effect of the anti-baby pills wear off.

Tomorrow, after I get paid, I'll send you at least $200. The car is safely in storage in Dallas. I'll have to send some more money for car payment and storage also.

It appears that everything I need to buy can be had here and I probably won't need too much.

For now I'll close, I still have some work to do before dark.

Thank you, Jacqueline, for your drawing to Daddy. I shall hang it up someplace soon.

Be patient on your "waiting, waiting, waiting." Time shall pass quickly.

Write as often as you can. Just a few lines, tell me what you do, etc. And everyone else can write in German.

I love and need you.

Love to you both.

Always,

Your Don and Daddy

3 September '67
Sunday 10:15am

Dearest Ruth and Jacqueline,

I have been very busy these last two days since we arrived in our new area. An Engineer battalion was here before us and they left some little huts/houses for us. Kind of like the garden houses in Germany. But a lot of work is necessary to make them good for office space, living in them, mess hall and storage areas. It's on the side of a small hill and the rain washes everything away.

So far everything is going real smooth. Everyone is working long, long hours and doing an excellent job. Our combat troops in "A," "B" and "C" troops are now starting to do their job and no one has been hurt or anything.

I've been flying about an hour a day mostly to get cool for a few minutes and get a breeze. It's just unbearably hot here. The water runs out of you with the least bit of effort and your clothes are soaking wet.

I'm trying to get showers fixed up so the men can get clean once in a while.

In the little villages or hamlets, as they call them, you wouldn't believe how sad, poor, dirty, hungry and sick the people look. Little children, of course, are always a delight and I keep thinking of our Jacqueline when I see them.

Once I have time and have my camera with me I'll take some photographs. I still haven't found how to get film developed. When I do I'll send off the 4 or 5 rolls I have.

I have millions of things to do honey, so I better get busy. I hope all is well and that you are beginning to feel better.

Kisses for you and Stinky.

For Now.

Love you, my darling.

Need you and love you.

Always,

Your Don and Daddy

3 September '67
Sunday 9:15 pm

Dearest Ruth and Jacqueline,

Today has been a real stinker, it has been so hot. It is pretty late and it's still around 98 degrees and 110% humidity. Our evening rain has yet to arrive.

It's been a long day and we managed to get quite a bit done. Our troops have been out on patrols and in the small villages protecting them from the VC so they could vote in their 1st Free National Presidential Election.

Except for minor actions they have been successful and have accomplished their job excellently.

I was up till about three this morning teaching how to properly keep operations, ongoing 24 per day so that everyone can get some sleep when necessary.

Had a shower made from an old 55 gallon drum and some pipes and that few minutes sure did feel good and for a just a little bit at least, I feel clean.

All is going smooth and I'm beginning to see some progress now.

I've been wondering and quite frankly worrying a bit about if you are okay, honey. I have been gone almost a month now and have had one short note in Texas and one letter from 22 August. I should think that at a minimum of 3 to 4 times each week you could write your husband. I don't care how many pages you write but just a short note several times a week would make my morale a hell of a lot better. Do try, will you??

I took my driver for a helicopter ride today and he was quite thrilled about it. Like I said yesterday, it's one of the few cool minutes each day.

How are you, my Jacqueline? Are you speaking English, I hope, and also your German? Behaving for Mommy? And having fun with your cousins?

You write me, you hear me, you big blonde bomber!

I love you so dearly, my darling. Want you, love you and need you.

Always,

Your Don

P.S. Kisses for you Jacqueline and your Momma only if she writes me.

6 September '67
Wednesday

Hello Blondies,

I have been rather busy these last two days and time just flew. Our troops are out searching for VC every day and return late in the evening - then small size patrols go out and stay all night till the first morning light. To support this day to day operation is quite a big administrative and logistical task.

Early Tuesday morning, Lt. Whitmore, the real baby faced one that escorted Col. H's daughter the night of our formal squadron party, was killed while out on patrol. One VC mortar round killed him and wounded very slightly 10 other soldiers. I mention this only so that you know I remain back in a secure base camp and it is our young lieutenants who are out on mission.

Yesterday morning I arranged for and we had a memorial service for him and an awards presentation by the General for the Purple Hearts and a Bronze Star for a very brave Medic who treated the men.

Except for this one incident that is all the damage so far to our men. They hunt and search each day and capture some but no major actions.

I spend most of each day inspecting, teaching and raising holy hell trying to get people to do things the right the first time. My staff is doing very well.

There is a continuous stream of higher staff, Generals and Colonels coming in each day by helicopter. They spend a few minutes and then fly off having made their combat trip for the day.

Mess halls, maintenance, paper work and construction keeps me busy.

About 12 midnight I go to sleep, take a cold shower from a big can, clean my equipment and sleep. Each morning a whole new day and different things to do come up.

Yesterday, I drove back to division headquarters to buy cigarettes and Coca-Cola. Both were out as Winstons and cokes are popular.

Today I'm going into a small village to arrange to build them a schoolhouse and each Sunday we'll treat the sick people, give children showers and try to help them. You would cry, Ruth, to see some of these people.

All is well with me and I'm working hard and feel I have done my job each day.

What is now worrying me to no end is why you won't write. Is something the matter? Are you and Jacqueline well? Do you have some problems that prevent you from writing a small two or three line note to me? Don't make it harder by not writing to me. Please! Please! Please!

I love you, I worship you, and I am always yours and spend many hours dreaming of you. Jacqueline, tell Momma to write me!

Love to you, both my Angels.

Always.

Your Don and Daddy

9 September '67
Monday 10:30 pm

Dearest Ruth and Stinky,

Finally since your letter of 23 August I have now received your letter of 1 September. Of course you must realize how happy I am to hear from you!

This "war" is a remarkable thing. Most of the day the Vietcong do not move against the people, but at night they are out and terrorize the small villages. Each and every day and night our soldiers are out searching and hunting them down-two or three at a time. We use all our ingenuity, firepower, strength, artillery and fighter aircraft to catch them. Our soldiers are very good, very brave and learn more each and every day.

We blow up their tunnels, caves, holes, capture their weapons, rice, ammunition and work like hell to kill or capture them.

It is absolutely amazing, Ruth. Just two kilometers off the beaches are high mountains, dense thick jungles, with no roads and only minor trails and little VC controlled villages. But every day by foot, by helicopter, by our vehicles we go in and rain hell upon them.

The weather is about 110 degrees all during the day and we are soaking wet from sweat. I guess we average drinking four liters of water per man per day.

In early October the rainy season or monsoons start where it rains at least 6 inches per day. Sun only about 2 hours and everything becomes a sea of mud and the roads wash away. This lasts about four months then good weather and then the spring monsoon starts.

I am working hard here in our base camp trying to get everything going smooth. We are feeding everyone 2-3 hot good meals per day, taking care of them as well as possible and working the hell out of them.

There is no relaxation for the men as there is no place for them to go. In the small villages they pass each day it is too dangerous to stay for too long or alone after 12 noon as they are "off limits." I have my wash done two times a week for about $1.50 each time. In a couple of weeks the squadron gets a movie projector and that should be some help for everyone.

I can't aptly describe this country. Perhaps when I get some pictures they will tell you more, honey.

Jacqueline, your Daddy thinks of you all the time. Yes, Daddy is on "maneuvers" and he loves you very, very much.

Tomorrow, one month of this year is finished. Only 11 more, my big Momma, and your big Daddy will devour you. I love and need and want you so much.

I am well, in good health, eat and sleep enough and work my tail off.

Please give Mutti my love and all the family and friends.

Please write me often, Darling.

I love you my Ruth.

Always.

Your Don

P.S. Greetings to all the Bowling Club friends.

P.P.S. Kisses to Jacqueline.

11 September '67
Monday 10:30 pm

Dearest Ruth and Jacqueline,

I received yours and Ria's letter of 4 September in "Wonderful Copenhagen." Glad you enjoyed yourself and have met some of the people. Ria's family sounds like very fine people. Some day we shall all travel and visit again.

Yes! Yes! Yes! My love, I miss you with all the love and passion I have. If you were here inside my bed and mosquito net, you would soon find out. Grrrrrrr.

Things are just busy as hell! Troops are going in 1000 and one directions trying to outguess, outwit, and catch the VC. A couple of days ago a patrol from Capt. Brown's "C" Troop caught hell but so did the VC's.

Today, a tank from Capt. Chris Conrad's "A" troop caught a mine and blew the hell out of it. I was in a chopper with Butch and Col. and we dropped down to pick up the wounded driver and evacuate him for medical attention. Nothing very serious, but the tank is a mess.

That is the sorry futile part of war. Little incidents all the time because the VC won't fight when the odds are against him. So we try to hunt him down and fix him and that is the hard part so far.

I am here at my base camp now after having been to visit every troop to see to their needs and wants. The men hold up well and are getting hard as nails.

This morning I bought four sets of plates and two vases for you to give to the family and friends as Christmas gifts. They cost me $45 for all. Local Vietnamese handmade wares. There is no such thing as a city here or a good store, just small, extremely poor, gypsy camp villages. So the selection is not like in a nice gift shop, honey.

By splitting up the sets as you see fit, everyone will have something from me. I'll look for something for you and Jacqueline as I can but I won't buy junk, okay honey.

Mosquitoes here are like Messerschmidts. Wow!

I'm just beat. I'm so tired, honey. I'll write again tomorrow. Kiss and hug Jacqueline from her Daddy. I love and miss my "Big Momma" so much.

Always.

Your Don

13 September '67
8:30 pm Wednesday

Dearest Ruth and Jacqueline,

Daddy is soaking wet! The monsoon rains are starting very slowly. I was flying down to "C" troop to see how Capt. Brown is doing and then went up to where Maj. Saint's S-3 is and drove back in my jeep in the rain.

Just a busy day with no major problems to speak of except I broke my lower partial plate last night and finally found a dentist today. He can't repair it so it required a new one. He took impressions and sent it off today. About five weeks or so and I'll have a new one.

I named my jeep "Viel Glück" (Good Luck) and took pictures of it today in honor of you and it goes with the lighter you gave me. Everyone asks me if it is Vietnamese. Ha! Ha!

Aside from heat, dust, rain, work, work and little else to do I'm in good shape.

Hope you are too as I sure do love that shape. Like to bite some sweet places. Grrrrrrrrrrrr!

Tis a short note, sweetie!

Write! Write! Write!

Kisses for Jacqueline from her Daddy.

Kisses to her Momma.

Love you

Always.

Your Don

15 September '67
Friday 8:30 pm

Dearest Ruth and Jacqueline,

Another short note and a quick one. For about three hours it has rained harder, longer and quicker than any rain I have seen in my life. Roads wash away, tents collapse, bunkers cave in. It is extraordinary and I just might add wetter than hell.

I set down with my chopper and dashed for my little house. The generator lights blew out and for a couple of hours I sat in total darkness just resting.

Our Commanding General has been working the hell out of us the last few days and it has paid off in some sixteen Vietcong we killed yesterday and today. A terrible high cost of dollars of equipment and men for each one we get. Lt. Barksdale's track hit a mine two days ago and made a mess but he was very slightly hurt and is back to duty today. Two tanks were also hit today. Keeps me busy trying to get new equipment, replacement soldiers, paper work, etc. Don't worry, I'm kind of like an inspector, as after it happens I go and find out how and why it happened and look for solutions.

You can do me a big favor, honey. Buy me a large rain jacket, rubber, with a zipper from a Fulda sports store and send it to me via airmail as quickly as possible.

I could also use a letter once in a while from you. My compatriots get them by the handful and I'm just empty-handed and sad.

The day hardly seems long enough for me to get everything done.

Honey, I close this quick note. I'm well, fat, healthy and love every inch of you. Kiss Stinky from her Daddy.

For tonight, I send my love.

Always,

Your Don and Daddy

19 September '67
Tuesday 10:00 am

Dearest Ruth and Jacqueline,

Hi! I've got a short break while I'm waiting for my driver to get back. Everything as I look out my door is like a sea of mud. It's damp, warm and little sun. Everyone is just working their tails off and things are going rather smooth today.

I just wrote my Mom and sent her our birthday wishes. Check and let me know Mom and Pop Filbert's birthdays. I don't remember them, okay?

What's new with you and Stinky? Are you having fun in Bad Orb with all your cousins?

Yesterday there was some kind of children's festival or holiday and in a nearby village just hundreds of them were all gathered playing games, exchanging presents, etc. I took some pictures. The kids were all so happy, but were in rags, hungry, needing so much.

Found $2.00 in my locker. Can't spend it here, so I send it to you to get Stinky a little something from her Daddy.

This is just a short note! I anxiously await mail delivery today for word from you.

Take good care of yourself and Stinky. I hope you are feeling better and no longer so nervous.

I love you my Big Momma and miss you, need you, want you.
Always,

Your Don and Daddy

19 September '67
Tuesday 7:45 pm

Dearest Ruth and Jacqueline,

After many days of feeling low and blue, I received your letters from 11 September and from 12 September. You can, I'm sure, realize what the few precious minutes of privacy reading your letters does for my morale. It takes me many thousands of miles away from here and I can almost see, hear and touch you both. It makes me happy and I can unwind the tension in me. Now when I sit alone in my little house, I read your letters again and again. I feel close to you these moments.

Each evening when I come back here my driver has the thing clean, my bed made, shoes cleaned up and I can relax for a while.

Today I am happy. The pictures you sent are great. Stinky looks so great with her big smile. I could just hug and squeeze her. You too, if I could get my hands on you.

You mention my shower. Oh! Yes, I would love to have you in the shower and later in my arms to love you and kiss and kiss you all over again and again.

Great! You spelled humidity right! Yes, I'm getting used to the weather. Ten minutes after a shower you get sticky and stinky again, the rain soaks you through and you just can't imagine it, honey. Right now it's raining so damn hard and our soldiers are out, awake and alert.

Daily spray for mosquitoes, two different kind of daily anti-malaria pills, salt tablets and once a week golf ball sized pills for malaria. What a place!

Today I made the rounds by chopper to visit everyone and on the way back an old Vietnamese man on a bicycle along the truck road was hit. The pilot was right down, we loaded him on a stretcher and in five minutes he was in our Army hospital. The helicopter is a lifesaver and the pilot saved one today.

I'm happy you're having no problems with the PX and commissary.
Dream nice dreams, honey!
I love you, need you, want you and am always,

Your Don.

For tonight I shall close. I'm happy because of your letters, so I will
sleep a bit better.

16 September '67
Saturday

Dearest Ruth,

Just a few lines. All is well just that I'm busier than a three-armed paperhanger. Tomorrow the squadron is conducting an operation and all the preparation plans have to be rehearsed.

We got a visitor yesterday, Col. Taylor, the ex-Chief of Staff of the 1st Armored Division who is now working in General Westmoreland's operation shops in Saigon. He flew up to see us and help with any problems we may be having. After six months here, he might get the Colonel, Butch and I a job or help us on a high level staff.

I'm doing the job of an Executive Officer (XO). The Colonel and Butch are concerned with tactical operations, but things are going just fine.

The rains I mentioned yesterday come like clockwork precision from 6:00 pm to about 8:30 pm. It rains like hell and then the rest of the evening a steady drizzle.

I'm still waiting to get the films back which I sent to the States to be developed. When I do, I'll send you some, honey. Perhaps you and Stinky can get one made for me and send it, okay?

I'm sure you're in Bad Orb with Jacqueline and all the children. Of course, I can't be sure, you write me so seldom. I thought by now I would have received at least a postcard from family and friends in Fulda, but no such luck.

I don't mean to bitch, honey, but it is one hell of a feeling to get only three letters in 45 days and everyone gets one almost every day from their wives.

1. Did you get the $50 bill in the letter I wrote from the boat?

2. Have you received the money orders for $300 I sent on 1 September?

3. Have you received the doll and cigarette lighter?

I was out checking our security a bit ago and I came back soaking wet. I've got a few other things to do. First of all, I'll get dry, clean up and just sit for a minute.

Hope you and Jacqueline have a good time. I love you both very dearly and miss my Big Momma and Stinky.

Will write tomorrow again. Love you, miss you and need you.

Always,

Your Don and Daddy

21 September '67
Thursday 10:00 pm

Dearest Ruth and Jacqueline,

Just a few lines this day. I've been busy sending you a surprise package that was hard to wrap. It should make you really happy, Jacqueline too, and me in return.

I'll have it mailed tomorrow and send it to the post office box.

All is well. Busy as usual, but doing real fine.

When your surprise package comes, follow the instructions carefully and you will have lots of fun.

Today I received your letters #2 and #3 and also got some pictures back from our visit in Dallas. Enclosed are some of them for you and Jacqueline and I have held on to a few. Particularly the ones of you in your bikini which got me all hot and bothered. I want you so much. Now, I wish you didn't have the bikini on when I took the pictures.

I was going to go to bed early tonight but those pictures of you in that bikini got me so excited, I'm like a bear. Those legs and sweet and prettiest boobies in the world make me want to love you and love you till I hear you moaning like you do.

I'll close for I want to take a shower (with you) and get some rest tonight.

Love to all.

I love you, miss you and need you, darling. Kisses for Jacqueline.

Always my love,

Your Don

26 September '67
Monday 8:30 am

Dearest Rutchen and Jacqueline,

I was so sleepy last night I just fell in the bed and couldn't muster up the energy to get up and write. Not lazy! Just pooped! It was a long day spent briefing some Colonels from US Army Armor School at Ft. Knox who were visiting us to determine how much maintenance is important for all our track vehicles.

Then, I spent the rest of the day visiting "C" Troop and raising hell with them. When I got finished, General Linnell landed and told Brown exactly what I just got through raising hell about. Brown's comment was "Guess Majors think like Generals and I still think like a junior Captain."

Didn't get time to send your pearls to you yesterday and/or today. But you should have them soon, honey.

Since we arrived here our Doctor and Medical personnel have now treated over 1,260 children for sickness, sores, infections and ills of all kinds. We have built a school and tomorrow there is a dedication service where the Colonel gets a medal from the District Chief. Ha! Ha! And he didn't even initially care about my project or even take an interest in it. But he is doing real good. He stays in the background and lets Butch plan all operations and I make all decisions and run things. I believe he does this to let Butch and I use our initiative, intelligence and learn. But I also believe he just doesn't know what's going on at times. Oh well! Of course, it would be a mess if he ran everything himself.

In a few minutes I'm going back to Division to take care of some administrative things for the squadron. It's about an hour trip by jeep.

All is well, my love. Still fat and getting real horny for you, as always.

Give Stinky a kiss from me.

Always,

Your Don and Daddy

28 September '67
10:20 pm

Dearest Ruth and Jacqueline,

Daddy has been very busy the last couple of days. I'm here at our base camp busy loading helicopters full of food, ammunition, radios and parts for Captain Staley's Bravo Troop who is out fighting very hard, very excellently and very bravely.

He has been out for over a week now and although he was wounded once has earned several medals for his cool and good control of artillery, mortars, jets, bombers, helicopter gun ships and his own soldiers. Kind of proud of him. Lt. Dickens was wounded twice in the last two days but just a few minutes ago the doctor said he was fine. I'll visit him in the morning.

I know you don't like to hear about this war, but nothing much else happens, nothing nice, nothing clean or pretty. And I am not fighting myself. I watch and that's all I do, or I listen and take care of papers, parts and people.

The squadron is starting to work real well, much safer and aggressive and our soldiers and officers are now catching the VC with their pants down and not the other way around. Capt. Staley must have gotten at least 125 in the last three days of hell he's been through.

Butch is doing an outstanding job and shows a lot of excellence. The Colonel remains the same, just a distant watcher who when he does say something, we spend the rest of the time trying to unsnarl his mess.

I'm fine, honey. Just miss you both so terribly.

Sent your pearls today, honey, and later I'll find more, and more expensive ones. They had some diamonds, too. If I can save some money or win some in poker, I'll buy the biggest one I can find for you.

Today your #5 letter from 21 September arrived. 7 days - not too bad a delivery time. When you say you have dreams about me, guess what? Then I have dreams about you that same night. I'm so horny for you, too. Grrrrrrrr!

Yes! Yes! Yes! When I come home Jacqueline shall have a brother! That's the first time you have ever said you want another.!

I love you and you shall have a son! I too, and Jacqueline a brother!

Poor Stinky, she is so little and can't understand why I'm not home. But you keep talking and let her see that I write words to her also.

Hello, Stinky. Your Daddy loves his fat little girl and he always thinks about you. Don't you worry because before you know, time will fly by and Daddy will be home. I love you.

Love Always,

Your Don and Daddy

DEPARTMENT OF THE ARMY
HEADQUARTERS AMERICAL DIVISION
APO San Francisco 96374

GENERAL ORDERS   11 February 1968
NUMBER   610

AWARD OF THE AIR MEDAL
(FOURTH OAK LEAF CLUSTER)

1. TC 320. The following AWARD is announced.

LUNDQUIST, DONALD C. 097939. MAJOR. ARMOR, United
States Army, 1st Squadron, 1st Cavalry APO 96374
    Awarded: Air Medal with "V" Device (4th Oak Leaf Cluster)
    Date action: 28 September and 29 September 1967
    Theater: Republic of Vietnam
    Reason: For heroism while participating in aerial flight. Major
        Lundquist distinguished himself by heroic action on 28 and
        29 September 1967 in the Republic of Vietnam, while serv-
        ing as squadron executive officer in charge of combat re-
        supply and support missions for troops conducting search
        and destroy operations. During that time, under intense
        enemy sniper fire, automatic weapons fire and mortar bar-
        rages, Major Lundquist directed the helicopters to the land-
        ing zones and personally aided in unloading the badly need-
        ed supplies on eight consecutive missions. Although he had
        one helicopter destroyed while it was on the ground and
        another one received numerous hits, Major Lundquist contin-
        ued to perform his duties with dedication and determination.
        When he observed that a medevac helicopter was receiving
        intense enemy fire while loading wounded personnel, Major
        Lundquist located the enemy position and called in accurate
        artillery fire which silenced it. Through his courage,
        rapid action, and determination, he contributed greatly
        in the defeat of the enemy forces, the saving of several
        wounded mens' lives, and the successful accomplishment of
        his mission. Major Lundquist's heroic actions and avid de-
        votion to duty are in keeping with the highest traditions
        of the military service and reflect great credit upon him-
        self, the Americal Division, and the United States Army.
    Authority: By direction of the President under the provisions of
        Executive Order 9158, 11 May 1942, as amended by Execu-
        tive Order 9242-A, 11 September 1942.

1 October '67
Sunday 8:45 am

Dearest Ruth and Jacqueline,

Hi, honey! Your Big Daddy misses you. I received your letter #6 from 23 September. Can't figure out what the mail delivery time problem is either. Your letters average 7 days. I can't see why mine take longer.

You just go ahead a put yourself in a package and mail yourself here. I can't wait to get to that box!

Last night I received your letter with the "happy family" pictures taken in Rhein-Main last February. Sure was a nice one of everyone just laughing and Jacqueline is a real "ham." I also received some snaps of the last couple of parades I was in, in Fort Hood. Kind of hard to see but I'm there. I've enclosed them for you to hold for my military scrapbook.

Your hope for peace in Vietnam is a good one. However, to the little people in the villages and to the soldiers, it is a dream. Peace will only be made on the highest level of political negotiation. Here in TamKy - Chu Lai provinces, they have been at war for almost 25 straight years. It would take us several years more and a few million more soldiers to permanently clear this area of the Vietcong. Like you, I wish for this "peace" also.

And I wish for the other piece too. I just vibrate at the thought of a kiss from you. Oh! Oh! Better change the subject, it bothers me. Whew!

The Colonel just called me and he is going to fly to Da Nang to pick up his brother who is visiting. He is a colonel who works for the CIA. Later when he returns, I will visit "C" Troop to handle some administrative problems.

Not much else is new here. Just work, sweat, stink, rain and work. Bravo Troop is back and in good shape.

I love you and miss you and need you, need you, you big blonde bomber!

Special wishes to Mutti, family, Rolbetzky's and other friends. Daddy sends you a big hug and kiss, Stinky. Love you both.

Always,

Your Don and Daddy

DEPARTMENT OF THE ARMY
HEADQUARTERS AMERICAL DIVISION
APO San Francisco 96374

GENERAL ORDERS   21 December 1967
NUMBER   1643

AWARD OF THE BRONZE STAR MEDAL

1. TC 320. The following AWARD is announced.

LUNDQUIST, DONALD C. 097939, MAJOR, ARMOR, United States Army, 1st Squadron,
1st Cavalry APO 96374
 Awarded: Bronze Star Medal with "V" Device
 Date action: 2 October 1967
 Theater: Republic of Vietnam
 Reason: For heroism in connection with military operations against a
          hostile force. Major Lundquist distinguished himself by ex-
          ceptionally heroic actions on 3 October 1967 in the Republic
          of Vietnam. On that date the base camp of the 1st Squadron,
          1st Cavalry was hit by intense enemy small arms and automatic
          weapons fire. Hearing the initial burst of fire, Major Lundquist
          ran from his quarters to the scene of the action, armed with his
          M-16 rifle. Major Lundquist detected a 6 to 10 man enemy
          force attempting to breach the barbed wire fences and immediately
          opened fire with his personal weapon. Disregarding the enemy
          automatic weapons fire and a painful wound in the neck and
          shoulder area, Major Lundquist moved among the friendly positions
          and directed their fire at known and suspected enemy locations.
          Major Lundquist's heroic actions were responsible for the defeat
          of the enemy forces and the protection of the Squadron's
          logistical base. Major Lundquist's outstanding display of
          heroism and his aggressive leadership are in keeping with
          the finest traditions of the military service and reflect great
          credit upon himself, the Americal Division and the United
          States Army.
 Authority: By direction of the President under the provisions of
             Executive Order 11046, 24 August 1962.

        FOR THE COMMANDER:

OFFICIAL: ROBERT H. MUSSER
                                   Colonel, GS
                                   Chief of Staff

DONALD Y. B. CHUNG
LTC, AGC
Adjutant General

3 October '67
Tuesday 10:50 pm

My Dear Dear Ruth and Stinky,

Hi Honey! It's late and has been a real long day here. Received your letter #7 dated 24 September from Bad Orb. Its been raining for two days off and on now and was cool most of the day with real hard winds coming off the South China Sea.

I got almost no sleep last night but rested a few hours this afternoon. Sometimes I check all the bunkers and guards to make sure they are on the ball. Last night they were not and it was a scramble for a while until they learned why they have to stay awake, be alert and do their job so everyone else can rest. Don't worry, nothing to speak of happened and all went well.

We all call where we at headquarter troop live "Fat City." It started as a joke and my energetic and humor minded Captain's had a sign made which is an absolute riot. We have so much fun with the name. Everyone who comes in here laughs .... that's good, for we need to laugh and smile every once in a while.

Enclosed are a couple of shots taken-this afternoon. Don't look too fat, do I?

Everybody got hungry in the middle of your letter. Me too! For you and a chocolate cake.

Yes! Yes! Yes! I want my Big Momma! Guess Jacqueline needs the closeness of you in bed. But will she adjust to it next year, honey? Poor thing, yes, but don't get her too dependent on you and have her tied to your apron strings. Still no word from Mutti, Lilo, Rolbetzky's .... just a card!

I'm well, tired and soooo! sleepy.

Love my Golden Girls.

Always,

Your Don and Daddy

4 October '67
Wednesday 8:00 pm

Hi Darling, You too Stinky,

As soon as it gets dark at night a lizard about a foot long comes up near my door and squeaks and chirps like a bird. I throw some candy outside or bread and then he is gone until the next day. Funny!

Not much new this day! We had some ceremonies at headquarters this morning for soldiers who won medals last month and then I came back here and slept a couple of hours this afternoon. Got soaked to the skin as I left my poncho here this morning.

We have all been working real hard lately and the monsoon weather is upon us now. The sun doesn't shine ... if it does, you can't see it for the clouds hang right on the ground.

Don't remember whether I told you Col. H's brother visited him the other day. Fine officer.

The plates and vases I sent are there, you say! How about the tape recorder and my tapes? And the Christmas package for you? Also sent Jacqueline one last week.

Ha! I mentioned on a tape they pay me $224 for flight pay, at least that's what I got this payday. Now today, they said, it was a mistake. We should have only drawn $110, so next month they take back $114 out of my salary. In November, we draw the normal $110 again. So sad! So sad! Too bad! Your Dad! Uncle Sam! Oh well, I didn't expect the extra money and $110 will help pay flight bills, car payments, etc. and will help finance and R&R trip which will cost a bit if I buy anything.

Guess you are back in Fulda now! What about getting an apartment?

Smile! Laugh! I miss you, love you, miss my Jacqueline and love you both. So So Much. Goodnight my Big Momma.

Always,

Your Don and Daddy!

7 October '67
Saturday Morning

Dearest Ruth and Jacqueline,

I've been busy and tired the last couple of days and didn't take time to write yesterday. It's been real quiet lately and the weather has turned a bit cooler and wetter! Rain clouds hang low in the air and it just rains and rains and rains.

There is always something going on to keep me busy and when there is not I go out and "stir the pot" so to speak, and make more work that needs to be done better. But most of the time I could really do very little and just get fat .... oh well, guess that's normal.

There is not much to tell you of recent only because each day is generally the same and repeats itself day after day.

I'm waiting for more pictures of you and Jacqueline which you said would send once back in Fulda. Better yet, I'd like a large, large one of you "playboy style."

How are you, Jacqueline? When are you going to start nursery school? Are you behaving like a little lady? I hope so! Did you receive your Dolly I sent you from Vietnam? If not, it should arrive soon. Remember Daddy loves you, Stinky!

All is well, darling! I need the very breath of you, I'm so lonely for you. To be at home, have a good meal, a cognac, and later a roll with you on the Persian carpet .... just wrestle you to the floor.... Oh how I need you!

I'll close this short note and wait for today's mail. Last couple of days no mail at all came in for the squadron.

I kiss you. I kiss you.

Love you.

Always,

Your Don and you too Stinky, Your Daddy

10 October '67

Memorandum to: My Rutchen

I know you don't like to hear about "war" but this clipping is about Capt. Staley's Troop and Lt. Dickens and it is real. It took place on 21-29 September.

Last night Col. Long (my old boss) called me. He is a Commanding Officer of an air cavalry regiment some 20 miles north of us. He just got here and is flying down to see me in the next couple of days.

The rain stopped today but the roads are all cut up. Received letter #10 dated 2 October today. I'm so glad you like the tape recorder ... it's a lot of fun and more personal.

I'm happy Stinky got rid of her rash. And it's good news that Mutti is feeling better too.

Received your tape of 6 October! The one where you mentioned that you are making a "love rug." Okay! We will christen it when I get home.

I wrote General Connor asking to get me to the Armed Forces Staff College next year. If he does it, then I'll get out of here a couple of months earlier. Keep your fingers crossed, honey.

Dear Stinky, I love you too. Just a note but I love you.

Always,

Your Don and Daddy
My thoughts are of you my two blonde ladies fair,
Happiness would be to see your Golden Hair.
And to see your smile and look of love divine,
Yet how happy I am when I know you're mine.

23 October '67

My Ruth,

Yes! I'm sure I'm in Vietnam's paradise. "Blackhawk Support" means we get food, ammunition, diesel fuel, radios, weapons and medical attention to our soldiers when they need it.

I'm the Mayor, the Ober-Burgermeister of Fat City. All my staff need a smile, a laugh and this Fat City name is now known all over this sector. Ask any helicopter pilot "take me to Fat City" and he knows just the hill where we are.

No ... I don't gamble too much, the stakes aren't high - only 25 cent games - and I make enough to buy pearls, etc. So, don't worry so much, honey.

Got two letters from you today and finally the tape where you acknowledge that you heard my tape that I got slightly hurt. Ruth, please don't worry. I told you, the little lucky Indian from Stinky, your love and my love is all I need to survive here. I'm just fine and will always be careful. And yes, I know you and Jacqueline need me ... I need you too.

Okay, now that is done ... you know ... I beg you not to worry about me ... for I don't run around here looking for medals or try to prove anything. I just do my job and my soldiers do the fighting ... not me.

I'm sorry Mutti is not too well. God is watching her, Ruth, so be big, strong, and brave and He will smile on her.

Today, I also heard from my mom, Sandy and Mark and Lt. Dickens who is in the hospital. He is fine again. I'll talk to you now on a tape, okay.

The pictures are bad but at least show you what the countryside looks like around here.

For now, darling, my love to you and Stinky. Kisses to Mutti.

Me too.

Always,

Your Don

Love you. Love you. Need you. Need you.

26 October '67

Dear Ruth and Jacqueline,

I love you both my Blondies. Be good to each other. Daddy is fine. He just misses his baby and Big Momma. I shall be so happy to get out of here, home to you both, a house, a home, a warm bed full of love, full of you, my Ruth. Your warm lips, heart, legs, bosom, bottom, and just everything for us ... we three, and then four.

You will have to bear with me for a while for as much as I miss the comfort of a good night's sleep, I know next year it will take time for the Big Daddy of yours to adjust again to warmth and peace at night. That is, peace and piece!

Love Always,

Your Don

28 October '67
Saturday

Dearest Ruth,

It is around four pm this warm sunny afternoon and I'm sitting here in my office and am so sleepy I can't keep my eyes open.

The strain of the last few days has been enormous and now I sit composing letters of sympathy for soldiers who were killed this last week. One of my distasteful responsibilities that makes me very sad.

Since 21 October "A" and "B" Troops have been fighting in a very bitter battle with the North Vietnamese Army (NVA). They have now killed several hundred Vietcongs and have been wonderful fighters. Captain Staley has been wounded, again and refuses to come back until they finish off the last VC. The soldiers and lieutenants have been so brave ... Lt.'s Kaeme, Bill Sheeler, Wallace. Although wounded they fight so strong.

No! I'm not with them when they are fighting ... I listen on the platoon and troop radios and hear every word. Once in a while, I'm up in a chopper at 3,000 feet above them with Butch and evacuate wounded, but Col. H and Butch spend most of the time airborne and I stay back and handle everything else. I don't like it, but that is they way it has to be ... either the Commanding Officer or XO must be in the Command Post. Both can't be gone.

I've sent you some clippings from the-newspaper ... not to make you sad, or worry, but because I'm so proud of these guys and I want you to know and understand what we are doing. Please keep them all in a special book or something so I can put them in my military scrapbook later.

The problems we have in Vietnam are so large and require a tremendous amount of sheer physical labor and plain hard work to solve. Every soldier and officer puts in so many hours each day and many, many days they just don't or can't sleep because of the things we need to do. I only have to tell them once ... I want something done, take care of this or that and it gets done in excellent fashion.

I'm fine honey. Just a bit glum in spirit and tired.

Received your tape with music, bells and the few words from you and Barbie the night you visited there. Ha! I enjoyed that very much.

Be back later Here it is 9:00 pm. I just got back by helicopter from a rush meeting with the Brigadier XO, S-9, and Aviation Officers over a minor flap as to how we can get choppers from combat resupply. Two hours of BS and one hour flying time. Problem solved! We got what we wanted and everyone is happy including my boss. But since he can't talk to Colonels or Generals without getting shook up, I do the talking and get results.

I flew close by "A" and "B" Troop and in total darkness they are still fighting VC in one hell of a battle. They are winning and that's what counts.

I missed supper and just had a ham sandwich, so I'm okay again.

Sorry I can't be jolly today, but I've been pressed hard these last few days, little sleep and I'm concerned for the Troops.

Keep working on that love rug. Keep sending me tapes and letters. Keep your good figure, big Momma. Keep on loving and needing me.

Love to you my Stinky. Daddy misses you.

Me too.

Always,

Your Don

29 October '67

Hi Honey!

Got your tape of 17 October today. I had to laugh when all the children were talking to me in English/German. And to hear them all laughing and screaming and singing ... it was so much fun for me.

And the food that Mutti cooked sounds just delicious. Next year I'll eat her out of house and home.

Okay, now that you have chastised me for being "lucky." Don't worry! I love you more than the Army. The Army has been good to me, but you're better, taste better, are warmer, give me more chills and thrills, make delicious food and love, the Army doesn't.

Oh! By the way, since we all may lose our flight pay the Army has approved 5.6% payraises, which means $49.00 more per month before taxes. The big one of $176 more comes with Lt. Col. which I hope to make on the outstanding promotion list next year.

It probably looks like I'm in a hurry to write. No! I'm just tired and have done so much paperwork and other things that I'm tired right now.

By the way, send me a big picture of you and Jacqueline together. Spend the $10, you tightwad!

Today I got my first Air Medal for some 25 hours flying time and 132 missions. Safest way to travel. No strain. I'm just fine, honey. By golly, time is flying by. Pretty soon three months will have passed.

Be big, be strong, be brave, be beautiful as always, be blonde, be pretty-bosomed, be pretty-bottomed, be biteable for me later next year, be best and for God's sake, don't fret .... I'll be back and I'll be a tiger, a lover, a good papa for Jacqueline and our yet to come "Michael Gordon Lundquist." I'll be good to you in the bed, on the rug, on the table, on the love rug, in the shower, in the hall, in the Mercedes, in the used Porsche, in the .... anyplace I want you ... and I do! I do! I do! Love you. Me too!

Always,

Your Don

2 November '67
8:30 am

Dearest Ruth and Jacqueline,

Good morning to you! I slept a little longer than normal this morning as I hardly slept a wink last night. Just couldn't sleep, that's all.

Now this morning it is raining like hell and everything is just a sea of mud. The weather is so bad that my helicopter can't fly in to pick me up .... so I've got a few minutes' time.

Yesterday I received your two packages of cakes and cookies and the coffeepot. I looked in the box, but you weren't in it. Poor boy! I thought for sure you would be there. Thank you and thank Mutti for all the cookies, I'll share them with the other officers.

Stinky still draws the funny people with arms and legs all coming out of their heads. That tickles me and I just laugh. Show her how to draw with circles.

I have been busy the last week doing just all kinds of inspections, coordination, raising hell, writing awards for people who have done brave things and good things, efficiency reports - you name it and I have done it last week.

My good friend, General Young, is here now and all I have to do is drive or fly back to Chu Lai, tell him our problems and he helps out immediately. Nice for a change. Prior to his arrival I thought the whole Division Staff was just "I don't care" lazy bastards, And they were fat and couldn't care less about the combat troops. But things are changing for the better now.

Perhaps today the troops will come back from an extended combat operation they were on. They need a day's rest, mail, pay, hot chow, maintenance and some good sleep. Captain Staley's troop has fought like tigers for the last nine days and won every battle they were in.

I don't think Colonel H is going to last much longer as Squadron Commander. He is starting to get all shook up and over the radio he goes all to pieces sometimes. Probably next month he will leave and we will get a new Colonel. Next month we will also start to shift some officers around from Command to Staff and vice versa. That way they all get a chance at command which is the best assignment, of course.

I really don't know what they will do with Butch and me after the Colonel leaves. They try to give all the field grades new jobs after 6 months ... so I guess we will just have to wait and see. They took $113 away from my pay this month, overpayment of flight pay again. Now, it seems that field grade officers cannot draw non-crew member flight pay at all, just the company grade officers. It was too good to be true ... so the hell with it!

Sent you the $400 on the 31st of October. I need very little so I'm okay. I have paid all bills to include tire payments, airline ticket payments, car loan and have no problems here with money. On 31st January, I start to draw the additional $360 that is now being taken out for the advance pay I drew in July. Then, I will save as much as possible and also have to save some for R&R money. Don't know yet, but I probably will still go to Australia. Hong Kong is having all kinds of political riots and uprisings, bombings, etc. Don't need any of that during my rest.

I'm real fine, honey.

Miss you so so so much Big Momma! Oh yeah! I'll be glad when this year is over.

Give Stinky a big hug and kiss from her Daddy.

Need, love, want, love, need, love, want YOU!

Me too!

Always,

Your Don and Daddy

3 November '67
Friday 10:30 pm

Hi Sweetie!

A long day just about gone! I just took an ice cold shower to wash away this day of dirt and grime. Man, was I dirty! I drove my own jeep about 60 miles as my driver is in the hospital with ringworm. I had it too, but I am better already.

I picked up an ABC News team by chopper and then three hours later had to go in and extract them. They used all their film ... so their day was finished. At $400 per week as a cameraman and the team chief gets $750. Yeah, yeah I, who takes them in and out. Oh well, who needs money? We do....

I put 7 hams in a chopper today, otherwise it would have taken me two days by jeep. The helicopter is the thing here. I saw 10 VC running and called in the Artillery on them and we got 6 of them and I shot one with my rifle, then set the chopper down and evacuated four of the wounded to our VC hospital. I'm being put in for a Medal, while just serving as a passenger, so to speak.

I already have 2 Air Medals, 1 Purple Heart, 1 Bronze Star, 1 RVN Service Medal with 2 Battle Stars, 1 VN Campaign Medal and the Colonel is putting Butch and me in for the Legion of Merit to present to us when he leaves in December. Got all I want in two/three short months and don't need any more. That's just the way it is here, Ruth, everything comes so quick to some sometimes, and I can so well remember the Korean War and I'm still trying to get the Army to award me two Purple Hearts for wounds from then. But God Bless them, all the witnesses are gone. But don't you get one gray hair on your beautiful head or elsewhere. Your Big Daddy takes good care of himself. Once was enough here! I'm always very careful.

I'm soaking wet ... I just ran outside in my shorts because a chopper was coming in with a message for me. Colonel H wants me to find out when he can go on R&R .... he is absolutely amazing! Butch and I as Field Grades have not even applied for one yet. Every other officer, yes, but we feel we can't go ... until ... the Colonel gets relieved. He sends a chopper down at 11:00 pm in the dark and pouring rain to find out when he can go on R&R. Oh my!

Tomorrow or Sunday I'm going to fly to Saigon to try to get replacements flame-thrower tanks, portable bridges and all kinds of equipment. It will be an experience, as I never thought I would get to see Saigon. We are so far North of there. I'll try to take some pictures, get to a PX to get something for Jacqueline for Christmas and will be back the following day. Col. George Hawley, my old boss from G-4 Wurzburg is Protocol Officer there and I will try to say hello during my short visit.

Wonderful angel! You! You! Now I have a coffeepot, tea, maggi, soup bullions. Ahhhh, wonderful. Thank you. I get violently ill and everything comes up when I drink coffee in the mornings. GI coffee is horrible. I heat water in your pot and make a cup of instant (I have a whole case free from the Navy) and later in the day or evening I brew up chicken soup and I'm in heaven. Not really, but close.

I'll be in heaven when I'm in you, kissing you all over, inside, outside, inside, inside till you come and come and come. AHHHHHH. I'm crazy I want you so much!!!!!!!

I'm glad you liked the pearl broach I sent you. It's a good one but I think it's more for an older lady. But hell, in twenty years you will like it. Right? Just teasing you.

I'll make a special tape and poem for Mutti's birthday next week and send it for you to play to her on her birthday, okay?

Best I get some sleep now, darling. Want to come to bed with me? No pajamas allowed, or in the daytime for that matter. I kiss your ears, your neck, your mouth, your most beautiful bosom in the whole world. Ohhhh, you make me crazy.

I play with you, kiss you for a long time, roll over on you, upside down and around each other we kiss. See! See what you do to me. GRRRRRR! I want you. I know I will dream about you in my sleep tonight and I hope you do too.

I love every breath of you, my Ruth

You are always my most loving truth.

I need you now and forever more and some

Because I am what I am because of what you have done.

What none could do before you my love

You mean more to me than any woman, you all above.

When I need you, you are there

In time of need, want, love and despair.

From the inside of you and that part of me

Just look at the comfort, love and joy you see

In our daughter, our product, our Jacqueline

It is God's love, my darling, we have seen.

Now in the days that we each other dearly miss

Shower our love on Jacqueline in Momma and Daddy's love and kiss

Squeeze her hard and always tell her about Daddy's love

Because it is the two of you I pray for up above. Now I know you are crying And I too, for my heart is sighing Just for you, for you, for you.

WOW! As you can see I miss you, Big Momma.

Be good to Jacqueline and I'll be good to the baby's Momma when I come home. 1, 2, 3, 4, 5, 6 times every morning, noon and night. Am I bragging? No, I've learned self-control. But no matter how many times, I still want you, need you, love you, respect you, proud of you, want and NEED YOU!

I love you. Me too!

Always,

Your Don & Daddy

P.S. Okay, I'll write you a love letter soon too, Stinky. Kisses for now.

11 November '67

Hi Darling!

I have just a few minutes time to write. Your Big Daddy is fine, well and strong ... just busier than hell. Today I received four letters from you from 31 Oct, and 2, 4, 6 Nov. They were soaking wet and two of them I could not read a word. Guess they got rained on somewhere before I got them.

I have been running around all the hospitals trying to find all our wounded soldiers from "B" Troop from their operation last week. I visited Dave Staley today and he is in serious condition but will live and in six months be good as new.

Well, we now have only 9 more months, honey. Sounds better each month now, doesn't it.

Thank you, Stinky, for the wonderful letters you write to daddy and also for your tapes. Tomorrow I shall try to write a long letter and also send a tape.

Our generator for electricity is broken for a few days. Hope it gets fixed soon because I need it for making your tapes.

Enclosed are some pictures from early in October taken from my jeep and helicopter. No new pictures of me, I'm waiting for another roll to come back.

Please don't worry, darling. I'm fine and just working hard.

I'll write again tomorrow.

Love you.

Always,

Your Don and Daddy

12 November '67
9:30pm

Hi Darling!

I just got back a few minutes ago by chopper and feel a bit better in spirits today, as things are going better. Spent all day with "B" Troop talking to every soldier looking at every weapon and vehicle after their last two weeks of extensive combat.

Their morale is wonderful, and I left Capt. Prothers there to get all the work done for their many medals for many brave soldiers. Perhaps Lt. Taylor will get a Medal of Honor out of the 9-10 November actions.

I visited Capt. Staley again today and although in very terrible pain, he is better. That poor boy has seen more in three months than many do in many wars. God Bless Him.

Col. H, Butch and I had a long, long talk today about what we will be doing in the next weeks and months. As it stands, Col. H expects to leave in December for a staff assignment in Saigon. Thank God!

General Young will help me to keep the squadron if I make this outstanding Lt. Col.'s list, but that would be too much to hope for. But I dream of that.

Got a bunch of cookies from Mom Filbert today ... all in small pieces (a spoon is necessary to eat them).

Yes, Big Momma. I dream of you too. ALL THE TIME in many ways of love and happiness.

Kisses for Jacqueline from Daddy. Greetings to everyone, family and friends.

I'm just fine, darling. No worry or fret. I'm just busy. But you know how much I love and need you, darling.

Love you both. Me too!

Always,

Your Don and Daddy

P.S. Kisses for you. Any special place?

15 November '67

Hi Honey!

All is well, just busier than ever. We are going 99 different directions and with missions it takes every bit of effort we can muster to get things done. As of this minute, most of our troops are not in contact, but preparing for some operations.

General Young, my friend from Schweinfurt has been to see me every day this week to discuss solutions to problems of support. We get along just great and I'm getting things we need a heck of a lot easier. Just a call him and it is solved.

General Connor wrote me and said my chances for Staff College next year are good. I'll know in December. If not next year, then the 69-70 school year. Let's hope it's next year's class. He also mentioned that Lt. Col. is no sweat. Just keep working hard and keep getting those tremendous report cards.

I'm safe and sound. Don't you worry about me, honey. I get frustrated at times here because mistakes cost such a high price. It's not like training, we cannot afford to make mistakes now.

I think of you constantly! There is many an evening I do not sleep for want of you, to talk to you, to hold you, to need, to love, to feel the warmth of you and the closeness of us. Miss our Jacqueline very much too.

This is just a note.

I'm fine.

I'm well.

I'm strong and I'm in love with you.

Always,

Your Don

C I T A T I O N

BY DIRECTION OF THE PRESIDENT
THE BRONZE STAR MEDAL

IS AWARDED TO

MAJOR DONALD C. LUNDQUIST, C97939, ARMOR
UNITED STATES ARMY

For meritorious achievement in connection with military operations against a hostile force in the Republic of Vietnam.
Major Lundquist distinguished himself during the period 12 October 1967 to 15 November 1967 while serving as squadron executive officer of the 1st Squadron, 1st Cavalry. In middle October, Major Lundquist was assigned the mission to construct,
build defenses for, and operate a squadron logistical base with
no combat protection forces to assist in its defense. Major
Lundquist built the base and successfully defended it against
repeated enemy ground action and mortar attacks. He rendered
continuous combat resupply, ground recovery and repair support
while under enemy small arms and mortar fire. Major Lundquist's
thorough planning and quick reactions to recovery, repair, and
resupply needs on the battle sites during ground attacks against
the villages of Ha Tay and Binh Yen contributed greatly to the
combat success of cavalry troops in the operation. Major
Lundquist's outstanding achievements and devotion to duty are
in keeping with the highest traditions of the military service
and reflect great credit upon himself, the American Division,
and the United States Army.

16 November '67
9:00 pm

Dearest Ruth and Jacqueline,

Just a few scant minutes ago I arrived back here at "Fat City" and am unwinding after a busy day visiting all the troops of the squadron and visiting the Col. and Butch for a few hours. All is as well as well can be here.

I went to see Col. McKenna for a statement about Lt. Taylor who we are recommending for an award of Medal of Honor action last week. Col. H was afraid to ask him so .... I went and told him what I wanted and he pleasantly and smilingly sat down and wrote for about a half an hour and was happy to do it for a very brave soldier. That's just a tiny example of Col. H not caring about his men. It's so bad, it's disgusting, Ruth. Oh well, he leaves soon, I hope.

Butch and I grit our teeth, humor him and then drive on to make the troops know we care, we are concerned and want things run, planned and executed well. They know it!

Me? I'm real fine, honey! A couple of weeks ago the strain of little sleep, dysentery, ring worm, work and frustration got me a little down, but after due consideration and more thought I have resigned myself to just keep working like I do ... and everything will work out okay. Guess it's best because things are going well in spite of him.

Generally, each and every day is the same for me. I spend a lot of time chasing all over the place taking care of things, leave the fighting to the troops and try to make sure they are always ready, get what they need, etc. This takes all my time, brains and energy.

Many, many times each day ... I day dream thinking of you and every time I do I get all kinds of warm thoughts of you and I love you so much darling. If I could somehow reassure you that you shouldn't worry I would ... for my love for you is so strong ... you are all I want. I'm not charging around here looking for medals or anything like it ... they just come in normal duty. Sure, every man would like to be a hero, but over here I have seen so many many brave boys who will remain here as heroes. Makes me think harder and longer now than I did before. I'll do my job and in a few months will be a staff officer in a safe place, pushing papers and pencils.

Mail has been skimpy lately. Hardly a letter for anyone in the squadron. But then it's great when it does come in.

I'll say goodnight now. You keep working on your love rug real hard. Think of me a little bit and remember how I love and need and want my big, blonde, Big Momma with the prettiest legs, bosom, bottom and oh so delicious mouth, tongue and lips and that oh so special part of you.

See what you have done now! I won't sleep for a while now I want you so much.

Good night my darlings! Kisses for Jacqueline and her Mommy too.

Love you.

Always,

Your Don and Daddy

22 November '67

Me dear dear Big Momma!

You made my birthday a very happy one ... far as one can be happy here. Your tapes, packages, gifts cards, photographs, well wishes did the trick. Last night I sat in the privacy of my hooch and read, looked, listened, touched, ate, drank and cried some too.

Thank you so, so much. The knives I shall wear on my pistol belt. They are just right, Ruth. I'm sorry about mail for you ... it is sometimes crazy here. Today I received letters from you from 7, 14, 16 November. Great!

Love the pictures of you. Hahahahahaha! And of Stinky, too, she is getting to be quite a big girl.

The Porsche picture you made is so funny. I just get tickled at your imagination ... love you my Ruth.

Damn it now! Don't you worry about me. I take good care of myself and next year I'll be there with bells on, happy and healthy and ready to try out our love rug day, noon and night. And this war will be all behind me and we'll be together again.

You look beautiful in those pictures at the wedding of Peter and his bride. Will you marry me, you beautiful lady? I should imagine that you would be a terribly exciting woman to make love to and be made love to by ... somehow I just think you would be completely different in bed. If you would care to experiment, then I'll rush right home.

I'm proud of you and more I cannot do than respect, love and adore you, which I do.

Please thank everyone who sent me greetings for my birthday. I loved them all.

Today I was very busy in "Fat City" because tomorrow is Thanksgiving Day and I want every soldier in the squadron to have an extra special good dinner tomorrow.

Only think and know how much I love you, my Ruth. Me too.
Always,

Your Don and Daddy
P.S. Jacqueline, your Daddy loves you too!

24 November '67
9:00 am

Dear Ruth and Jacqueline,

Daddy had too much to eat yesterday as it was Thanksgiving and we had a turkey with all the trimmings. I invited Col. H down to see "Fat City" and then we ate, got back in the chopper and visited all the different troops while they had their meals.

I spent close to four hours flying from here to there and back again. It was kind of an easy day, but I was still a bit tired last night.

The enclosed picture was taken out where Bravo Troop has its base camp, and I was just coming out of Capt. Baronetto's tent. Not a good picture, but you may want it.

Today promises to be a busy day ... this I like ... for the time passes quickly then.

All is well, darling. I'm fine and as healthy as a young stud.

Still busy with lots of paper work for all the medals the soldiers are winning, but I generally do this in the evening hours when I can write and not be interrupted.

Now that Col. H has made the outstanding Colonel's list .... which we doubted was possible ... perhaps there is hope that Butch and I can make the outstanding Lieutenant Colonel's list. This is the first time I'm in a zone for outstanding and have a chance based on some real great report cards. Oh I hope so, honey!

All is going real fine. None of our troops has been in contact with the NVA or VC in the last ten days ... so they are all in good shape, men are rested up and the equipment has been worked over.

Hope all is well at home. Hug Mutti for her birthday and give our little Stinky a real big kiss from her Daddy.

I love you, miss you and need my Big Momma.

Love. Me too.

Always,

Your Don and Daddy

27 November '67

Dearest Ruth and Stinky,

All is well, I'm just physically worn out. I'm now up three days —no sleep - and finally things have quieted down again.

Butch is in Saigon on a briefing mission to Headquarters and I've been doing his, mine and the Colonel's job, in some recently busy operations. I enjoyed doing everything but I'm just pooped tonight. No energy to send you a tape. Tomorrow I shall, sweetie.

Gosh darn it, don't worry about me. I can and do take care of myself. I've got all the luck in the world behind me. You and Jacqueline! More, I couldn't use.

I got Col. H and Butch Air Medals with "V for Valor" approved the other day and the Col. has put me in for a Distinguished Flying Cross and Bronze Star and Legion of Merit and yet another Air Medal! Do you see what I mean? I'm not looking for anything but getting my tail out of here safely - and it comes to me.

This war may be unpopular, and not even understood by you or Europeans or Americans or British, you name it, but the commitment of National Policy to save the Vietnamese from attack by Communist takeover of SE Asia is being upheld to our best efforts. The same as would be done under NATO agreements.

Releasing a Vietnamese family from VC control after 11 years was just one experience I had today! I photographed the mother and two children in a village we liberated. I cannot express the joy, relief, and thankfulness that mother displayed. I hope my camera did. You can understand this, I'm sure.

Honey! I don't need anything. When I do, I'll holler real loud, "I NEED YOU." Okay? What then? Mail yourself to me?

Stinky, Daddy loves your letters too. Especially the ones with the all of Daddy's stars. First Daddy will just be happy to make the Lt. Col.'s list, then General. Love you my Stinky.

You had better prepare yourself for "no late night movies" for you shall not have energy left. This I guarantee you, Big Momma. Till tomorrow's tape.

I love you. Me too.

Always,

Your Don and Daddy

30 November '67
9:00 am

Hi Sweetie,

Been sitting here writing checks and sweating over balances like I do every month.

As you can see from the attached expense list, your money and what I draw across the pay table, I've been a bit lucky each month at poker and have been able to kind of make up the difference from what they are taking out for the advance pay. The end of January will finish that up, thank goodness.

We pay $30.30 for our meals each month here. Not bad, but I think they should be free. Oh well.

And for the next three months they are taking back $50 for Flight Pay they first approved, and then decided we weren't really eligible for. The dirty dogs ... Oh well, again.

I hope that with your expenses you are able to save at least $75-100 per month. Are you? I hope so ... It would be great to have a little bit saved up and then when I get home we are going to buy the best, biggest and most luxurious bed and bedroom furniture because I intend to keep you in it.

Butch brought back some of your tapes from Saigon today. So I'll make some tonight.

I've gotten letters from the Rummels, Dianne's parents and the Schwarz's in Auburn, all of which I have to answer yet. Fred and Dianne sent all kinds of cheeses, oysters, kippers, sardines, etc. Hope I can eat all the stuff I've received.

Tell Jacqueline that her Daddy sent her a little gift and that he loves her too.

Hope your cold is better. All is well, I'm fine ... just terribly lonesome for you and Stinky.

Love and need you. Me too.

Always,

Your Don and Daddy

PS - So that you see I've been a bit lucky each month:

Dinner's Club (Air ticket)	$ 14.61
Carte blanch (air ticket)	$ 28.84
Gulf Oil (tires)	$ 23.10
Dial Finance (loan)	$ 56.00
Car Payment	$ 120.00
Fastcolor (pictures)	$ 3.21
Kodak (film)	$ 4.00
Harlinger Bank	$ 100.00
Car Storage (Dallas)	$ 30.00
	$ 384.76
Drew on payday	$ 451.00
I have	$ 65.00
You have	$ 400.00

That means I paid the bills with the winnings.

I thought of something I want. Go to a professional photographer and get a large color photograph made of you and Jacqueline. Please. Please.

2 December '67
6:00 am

Dearest Ruth and Stinky,

Goodness! I hope you are feeling better by now, my Big Momma. I don't like that you're ill. Take care of yourself and feel better.

I've been awake all night long and I'm too sleepy now to go to sleep. I ran an alert tonight to practice security and everyone else is awake too. I'm not being mean, it just has to be done to keep them on their toes.

Ha. Ha! Don't worry so darn much, my ringworm is almost 100% gone. I look like a boiled lobster and I just have coated myself with iodine. Every day it's a little bit better.

Been working hard lately and I haven't had too much time for myself and I've just been too pooped at night. It's pitch black outside even though it's 6:15 am and it's raining like hell. We are back in the monsoon rains again and at least half the day and night it's raining.

The squadron is fine. People are working and doing well.

Thanks for sending the promotion list. Lt. Col. H will be a full Colonel soon. Will wonders never cease.

Soon I'll get some coffee and breakfast and then, I hope, I'll wake up.

My Big Momma and Jacqueline, your Big Daddy misses you so much that it hurts inside. Pretty soon now, it will only be 8 more months to go. How about that? Great!

I love you darlings.

Kisses and squeezes to you both.

Love you.

Always,

Your Don and Daddy

4 December '67

Hi Sweetie!

Today I did virtually nothing except sit inside my hooch, write a couple of letters, clean up some paper work and mostly rest. The reason? Because no choppers could fly as it has been raining continuously all day and you can't see more than 100 meters up, down or sideways. Wow!

I finished up some awards I was writing and then spent a wonderful couple of hours listening to a your tapes once again. Kind of makes me happy, sad and all choked up inside to hear your voice and Stinky's. God, I miss you both.

Tonight ... just before supper a package with your advent candleholder and Jacqueline's pictures of Santa Claus arrived. This makes my day complete. I think I'll sit down and cry or have a good snort of Cognac. Oh well, it's just this Christmas ... but my heart and deep love are with you both.

I mailed all the Christmas cards today and wrote several letters so I'm all caught up for a while.

My Rolex watch started to gain time at an unbelievable rate. Sure would be nice to rotate out of here based on my watch. It gained a whole 24 hours each 24 hour period. That would mean I'd be out of here four months sooner. I sent it to New York for repairs today. In the meantime, I'll use an Army watch, which I have plenty of.

Soon I shall get busy and stop being so lazy in order to properly get things in shape for the new Colonel's arrival and Col. H's departure on 1 January '68. I hope to make an impressive "Change of Commission" ceremony for them both. My duty ... I'll be glad when it's over and hope the new one assumes his rightful position with some drive, imagination and leadership. If so, it will be a welcome change, as you know.

All is well, Big Momma. I love every inch of you and wish I could just do that with every inch of me. I love you. I miss you and please send me you for Christmas

Jacqueline, you be good and Santa Claus will come soon.

Goodnight my sweeties. Love and need you. Me too.

Always,

Your Don and Daddy

6 December '67

Hi Honey!

All is well as usual. Today just a short note as I'm tired of writing ... been at it most of the day again.

Since a new Colonel comes at the end of December, Christmas is coming for the soldiers and numerous officers are being switched to new jobs before Col. H leaves, there is lots of new work to get done for me. This I like because it keeps me busy and time passes more rapidly.

Today I received another package with an advent calendar and those precious little dwarfs from Jacqueline. This Saturday I will light the 1st Advent Candle with you and think of you both, my extra special loves.

I'm happy you finally go to the movie theatre now. That's good for you. I should like to see Dr. Zhivago myself. But no movies here.

I am very sad to hear about Mutti and I pray that she holds on and will have a wonderful Christmas this year with her children and grandchildren. Although I am not there, I'm sure you will make her know I send my special love to her. Of course, I will send her a Christmas tape.

We are now starting to get some new officer and soldier replacements. Every day two or three more come in, so the change in scenery is beginning. Col. H goes to Saigon and will be doing G-1 work, which he knows nothing about, so it should be a good experience for him ... to have to work, that is.

I imagine that about 1 March both Butch and I will move on to new jobs in other units or a staff assignment some place. By that time, we will both be ready because these last months have taken a lot of energy out of us. Not so tired really but it's hard to keep our interest high. Change is good.

We started yesterday back under the operational control of the 196th Light Infantry Brigade who moved North into our area of operations. General Linnell used to command it and we got along just great. He has since left and an Armor Colonel is its new boss.

In just a few short days the new guy has created all kinds of problems, people at each other's throats, distrust and a mass of confusion in all the battalions under his control. Poor Butch and Col. H are going nuts. Me? No sweat ... I can work for anyone. But this guy is just scared to pieces and I guess it will take lots of time before he knows what or how to do things right. That's the hard part ... we do know and have been doing great all along. Thank you for the wishes on the Medals. As I told you, since then I've been put in for three more. A Bronze Star for Valor, a Legion of Merit, two more Air Medals, one of which is for valor. No. sweetheart, I'm not charging around looking for medals.

A great big hug to you and kiss my Stinky and the baby's mother too. Enclosed are some pictures. More to follow soon.

Love, need, want and miss you.

Always,

Your Don and Daddy

8 December '67
11:00 pm

My Big Momma,

Hi Sweetie! Just a short note this date. All is well but I've been busy and had a long hard day with a million things to do.

Butch and I have been out inspecting and relieving people all morning. Just lazy sargeants ... no officers ... but soon Captain Brown will get relieved if he doesn't shape up his people. The three Generals are all after him. He fights like hell but that is all.

Got your letter of 1 December today. I'm glad Stinky's package arrived and you think it will fit our fat little sausage. I'm sorry I can't send things to everyone and I would have liked to have sent you something special, but I will make it up to you upon my homecoming, Sweetie. You know I love, need, miss and want and want and want you.

Don't worry about my medals. I just sent them home so they wouldn't get wet, ruined and all wrinkled up. Since then I've gotten two or three more. I'll send them next month when they are awarded to me. Just put them someplace and I'll figure out what to do with them later.

Got some more pictures back today. I've enclosed the good ones and gave some soldiers and officer ones of them I had taken.

Four-Star General Westmoreland came to see us yesterday. He was very impressed and said if every battalion had killed as many VC as we had these last six months this war would be over in one year. Took some pictures of him and me. He is a genuinely handsome gentleman and appears rather calm, but sharp as a tack. Col. H did a poor job of briefing him, but that's normal.

I guess I'll get some sleep now. Will be dreaming of you, around you, between you, in you, bottom, top, upside down, aside, along, in between ... Oh My!

Goodnight my Big Momma. Kisses to you, Stinky.

Love you both. Me too.

Always,

Your Don and Daddy

11 December '67
Monday

Dear Honey!

Today has been an interesting day and it's still early afternoon yet.

Remember the picture of the school I said we built, well 3 days ago we added another wing to it and early this morning a VC squad came into the village and blew it to pieces. So, we are starting to build again. This illustrates just some of our frustration here.

We received several hundred Christmas cards from 6th grade students from all over Ohio expressing their love for us and their faith and wishes of strength in the American ideals. I've taken time to have long letters written for each child who writes. The kids address their cards to: Army Soldier, 1/1 Cavalry. It's very heartwarming to say the least.

General Young flew in here to see me for lunch and I solved many of our support problems. Gee, it's great having him as a friend because he loves this squadron now.

In a few minutes I'm going up to Division to further help solve some parts and equipment problems.

Things are starting to get rolling for Christmas. Packages are coming in from organizations all over the world for the men. We got special decoration kits for mess tents and just all kinds of other goodies. No man will not have a present or a personal touch and feeling of concern from home.

Me? Oh, I'm fine as usual, just my hair is growing over my ears, no time to barber lately. I'm still fat and pudgy (not really), but tired as hell, frustrated as hell sometimes, but generally in good spirits as each night I sleep well knowing I've done a day's honest work.

The hard part of every day remains the few hours at night that I read your letters, listen to your tapes and lie there thinking about my beautiful wife and daughter.

Since it's 11 December, another month is gone. Isn't that great? I think so. Before you guys know it, I'll be in both your arms again. Happy days again! I'll finish this note tonight, sweetie.

It's now about 6:30 pm and my trip to Division headquarters was profitable in that I got some things done for the squadron. I was happy, a letter from you with some more pictures of my Blondies arrived. You both look great in your boots. I love Jacqueline's hair ... so long now...and she just keeps getting bigger. Whose poodle is that? Ours? If so, I like it. Did I ever tell you how sexy your legs are? Grrrrrr.

Yes, I have received the Advent's packages and I eagerly await the repair of your tape recorder.

What else is new? Not much really. Same thing every day. My adrenaline always pumps the same rate ... fast and I'll be glad as hell when this is over.

How is your Mutti? I do hope that all remains well through Christmas. Please give her my love.

I've got some paperwork to do yet, sweetie, so I'll close for tonight, but not before I tell you I love, want, need, and miss you my sexy Ruth and our sunshine, Jacqueline.

Always,

Your Don and Daddy

P.S. The small pleasures of my job. Lt. Barksdale's wife sent me this thank you note from getting him his R&R.

November 30, 1967

Dear Major Lundquist,

Thank you so much for handling our R&R with such magnitude! Because of you, what once was to be, now shall ever be. You may think that your part was "no sweat" but I consider your careful maneuverability as supreme and powerful, worthy of great praise and thanksgiving. All these things being relative, what you might have thought was a deed in a day full of many jobs and responsibilities turned out to be my answer, which is to say that you have moved the world as far as I am concerned. So thank you very much, Major. And I'm looking forward to seeing you again so I can thank you personally. And you can be sure that we appreciate your help and will think of you in HAWAII!

An admirer always,

Gayle Barksdale

14 December '67

Hi Honey!

Busy, busy, busy the last two days. Just work, that's all. Trying to get all our shot up and blown up tanks back together again.

Butch leaves the squadron on 15 January to become Deputy G-3 to the G-3 of the Americal Division in Chu Lai.

General Young said to Col H that on 1 March he is making me the G-4 of the Division. That's a Lt. Col.'s job! We shall see. I'll take it if they ask me. Have no worries!

You won't believe this, but I've got on long underwear, a sweater, a tanker's jacket and I'm still chilly. Temperature dropped from 105 degrees to 58 degrees in one day. It's raining like hell, windy and whew! I'm cold.

I'd love to see snow instead. Glad the money arrived. Buy what you want honey, but don't go crazy.

Tomorrow I'll make a tape and send it off for Christmas.

I love you, my Big Momma. You too, Stinky.

Me too.

Always,

Your Don and Daddy

17 December '67
Sunday Night

Dearest Ruth and Jacqueline,

All is well and quiet as I sit here in a few stolen moments by myself. The Advent Candles are burning and my thoughts are completely with you, of you and about you both.

It is so lonely for me at times. Like now, and I so terribly miss you both. It would be so nice and wonderful to be there with you.

Today I spent five hours flying in a combat mission with Butch, and we both killed a large number of VietCong from our helicopters ... it just simply gets to me sometimes. I came back tonight, completely empty inside ... not just because of killing people, but the whole bit ... our hurt soldiers, the local people who live in terror of the VC and the VC themselves. Sometimes I get so worked up inside I'm like a volcano. But enough of that ... it will all work out of my system later ... much later, but it will disappear in time. It's just so sad.

How is my Stinky? Are you happy that Santa Claus is coming? Was St. Nicklaus good to you on December 6 or did you get coal in your boots?

Tomorrow Bob Hope, Raquel Welch and a bunch of singers put on a show in Chu Lai. I hope to see it. Last time I saw Bob was in Korea. I'll take some pictures if I get to the show.

Ruth, I'm well and strong and fine ... just busy, tired, sad, lonely, and miss you and Jacqueline so, so, so much.

My love to my sweet Momma.

I love and need you.

Me too.

Always,

Your Big Daddy, Don and Daddy

22 December '67

Dearest Ruth and Jacqueline,

I rush this note to you. Busy as a beaver. The Chief of Staff of the US Army, General Johnson, was here all morning. I'm leaving in a few minutes to be President Lyndon B. Johnson's "aide" on a tour of Vietnam tomorrow morning. Why me? I don't know.

I hope to be back here with the squadron in the next couple of days.

I'm a bit excited, sure. First General Johnson this morning, then the President tomorrow morning.

Proud to be going. Will write about it ASAP.

Love and Merry Christmas, Darlings.

Always,

Your Don and Daddy

23 December '67
1900 hours

Dearest Ruth and Jacqueline,

Got back an hour ago from one long night and day of no sleep and am tired now. All morning I was in Cam Rahn Bay north of Saigon with almost 2,000 other officers and soldiers to see, hear and talk with President Johnson. Every Three and Four-Star General in Vietnam was also there.

For 2 hours we saw, listened and talked with the President. I was just about three feet from him and took some pictures. After awards ceremonies, speeches, hand-shaking and Christmas wishes, he left for America.

I then flew back to Chu Lai and gave a report to the Chief of Staff and then flew in here.

It was a nice experience and everything and I was proud to have been selected to go, but I'm just so tired. No sleep, inspections, standing all day and waiting, etc.

Tomorrow I have a busy day and will visit every soldier in the squadron and give them a gift and wishes. I'll write and make a tape tomorrow night. Now I'll sleep a bit.

Love to my blondies,
Your Big Daddy and Daddy

P.S. Always. Me too.

24 December '67

Christmas Eve

Dearest Ruth and Jacqueline,

    MERRY CHRISTMAS!!!

    As this day closes, my eyes are a bit misty for the loneliness of Xmas '67.

    I have flown in a helicopter almost nine hours delivering a present to every soldier.

    It has rained all day ... my helicopter has 11 holes in it ... no, none in me. But we had a little Christmas for every man, and that is right.

    I can only say I love you both and miss you so, so dearly, my first time away from you in seven years.

    My complete heart is with you.

    Love you.

    Always,

Your Don and Daddy

25 December '67
Christmas Day
To Be Opened On Christmas Eve
Christmas 1967

To Ruth

Ruth, my love ... in all your hearts despair,
Smile wide ... for I feel I am really there.
There to share in the warmth of our family of three,
Beneath the simple beauty of that Christmas tree.

Tho' the miles be so wide and distance great and far,
Look high at that gleaming star.
I close my eyes and with magic I can touch,
Your cheeks of tears and your love that means so much.

Above all riches that I can possibly give to thee,
It's my love, I send, look high, it's on the Christmas tree.

Christmas 1967

To Jacqueline

Jacqueline my child so fair, you're sure to see,
Sweet things and joy around the Christmas tree.
The things you can touch, see and feel
Are not important, for it's the spirit of Christmas that is real.

Look high to the top of the tree ... there shines a star,
That is your gift from me, from way afar.
And more than all things, it shines from above,
With its real warmth and true meaning ... it's your Daddy's love.

26 December '67
13:30 pm

Hi Big Momma,

I'm waiting for my helicopter to come in so I can visit with the Colonel on some paperwork. Today is nice, it's warm and the sun is shining. Yesterday, on Christmas, it rained and was cold all day. The VC are quiet today, so far. Even though they violated the truce yesterday, no one was hurt in the squadron. Every soldier ate a good meal, got two extra cans of beer or soda, a small gift from the people of America and they were in good cheer.

Me? Oh, I'm fine. Yesterday I felt just awful and sad, but it made me happy to think about Jacqueline being happy and all the family in Bad Orb. Next Christmas will be a happy, happy one for me.

Now I'm starting to get things ready for the new Colonel's arrival on 2 January. We will have a very short "Change of Command" ceremony, some Medals awarded, goodbye presents and then get back to work.

I'll save some talk for the tape I will make later this evening.

Sure! That sounds nice, why don't you go skiing in Switzerland with Ulli. You don't have to ask me, honey. You go and get brown, slim and get your legs in shape to go around me when I get home.

For now, Sweetie and Stinky, I love you!

Always,

Your Don and Daddy

27 December '67

Hi Sweetie,

About 11:30 pm. I've been awake most of the night and now just took a fairly warm shower to cleanse my dusty, dirty old body.

Days like this are long and hard sometimes. Not the war particularly...but just all the things in general. Ya! Ya! Keep my chin up, head down and smile. Okay, I'm smiling.

Enclosed are a couple of pictures from Chief of Staff General Johnson's visit last week. More to follow when my pictures get developed.

Enclosed are also orders for my

1. Bronze Star for Valor
2. Air Medal 2nd Oak Leaf Cluster

I'll send medals and certificates after they present them to me on Saturday.

Another Bronze Star for Achievement is still being held. Chances are not too good, unless Col. H talks to the General.

And Another Air Medal for Heroism, again, not too good unless Col. H gets in the act.

And still Another Air Medal will be approved, no sweat, in January '68 for hours in combat in the air.

And yet another Distinguished Flying Cross for Heroism just went in. Chances are not too strong. But who knows what these award boards think is brave or just duty back in their safe headquarters.

Still busier than hell, what with Col. H leaving (thank God), the new CO. coming in, combat, many changes of staff and troop commanders, and just simply teaching everyone how to blow their nose and not their new jobs. Woe is me ... always work. Now I believe that being a Major is the Army's the most worthless rank because you do just all the work, all the time.

Oh, hurry up and make me a Lt. Col.

Ya! Ya! The list comes out soon. Pray, Big Momma, just one outstanding promotion or it's another two years for regular promotion. Just once!

I've got so many things to do to get everything done. Kisses for my Stinky!

Daddy loves you both so, so much.

Goodnight my blondies.

Me too.

Always,

Your Don and Daddy

31 December '67
New Year's Eve
8:00 pm

Hi Sweetie,

I've been busy today ... the new Commanding Officer, Lieutenant Colonel Walter C. Causland, 35 years old, West Pointer, Class of '53 came in Americal today and comes to the squadron tomorrow. I had lunch with him today and I like him. He is older looking, sensible and appears interested in doing some work himself, which will be a change.

Butch leaves 15 January and yesterday we got a replacement, Major Medberry a reserve officer, very junior type, 34 years old, who has never been in a Cavalry unit, admits to knowing nothing but is willing to try.

Because of this I will probably take a more active part in operational aspects of the squadron, at least until he gets oriented and the new colonel learns the ropes too. I'm looking forward to the next couple of months as new, keep real busy times - Why? Makes time go faster!! And I believe the new CO will do a good job.

Like a good X.O., I went to every General and just for the image of the CO. leaving his squadron, wrote and signed and got approved for Col. H

a Silver Star (Heroism) "Joke"

Legion of Merit (Achievement) "Joke"

Air Medal (Valor) "OK"

Air Medal 3rd and 4th Clusters "OK"

Vietnamese Cross of Gallantry "Joke"

I mounted captured weapons and swords on a wall plaque and mounted spurs and certificates as gifts.

So this pitiful old Colonel will leave here with tears and great emotion and perhaps believe that he is the greatest!? But ... be that as it may, it is a good XO's job.

Me? I got another Maximum Report Card and many works of outstanding written praise, which is what counts. Plus, I'm in for some more awards, too.

I like Col. H, but just think he is old, lazy and coasting on a dream staff of officers. Can't blame him, that's his rue to remember and everyone of ours, too. C'est la guerre! Tomorrow at 4:30 pm, for the first time in five months, as many officers as possible are going to gather for a "New Year's Drink."

The following morning a "Change of Command Ceremony" and then off we go again.

As in a few hours the year 1967 passes, let me say you have been a patient, wonderful, loving, understanding wife and I love you for this.

In the New Year of 1968, we shall see the three of us together again, in each other's arms and happy once more. It's only 219 more days, maybe less if I'm on the school list.

As the old year goes out and the New Year comes in, I shall sit here with my candle, a whisky and kiss the thought of you, my love. I hold you tight and tell you in your ear ... "Me too."

Always,

Your Don and Daddy

PS. $567 paycheck this month (includes $46 pay raise)

-$200 for you

-$119 car payment

-$ 56 loan

-$ 30 uniforms

-$ 18 Jacqueline's books

-$ 23 car tires (last payment)

-$29 Carte Blanche (airline tickets)

-$15 Diner's Club (airline tickets)

-$ 30 car storage

-$ 30 Harlinger Bank

$548 total

$18 for me! I didn't play poker this month....

Next month I get $350 more.

THANK GOODNESS!

3 January '67 oops '68

Dearest Ruth,

I'm fine, just busier than can be. The Change of Command was just outstanding in every way and, of course, many compliments were received for my outstanding ceremony.

I succeeded in bringing Col. H to tears with his many decorations, gifts and things. He left ... and then the strenuous task of briefing the new CO. began.

I did not sleep for two days, we were so busy and he is off to a fairly good start having all the background information he needs.

Butch is leaving in about another three days. The Generals and Chief of Staff asked me when I want to leave the squadron. I, of course, am ready now but will probably stay at least a month more. I'll keep you posted, honey.

Received a tape from 20 December yesterday. Enjoyed it.

Now that the holidays are gone, I'm happy not to have the sadness of the holidays alone to face any more.

Love to my blondies.

Me too.

Always,

Your Don and Daddy

P.S. Some medals I won are enclosed.

7 January '68

Hi Sweetheart.

My heart is heavy today as the last few hours here have been hard. I have been listening on the radio as the troopers of "B" Troop have bravely beaten back suicide attacks by North Vietnamese Battalions attacking their positions at LZ Ross. God Bless Him, but John Baronetto, the troop CO, was killed. He was the prematurely grey haired ex S-2. I recently sent pictures of him.

This war is just hell, darling! Me? I'm alright, have no fear. I just feel crushed inside since I talked to John this morning and he was such a brave soldier. Lt. Wheeler took over in combat and did magnificently.

Butch came back to "Fat City" with me tonight and he leaves in the morning for the G-3 job at American in the morning. I will miss him as he is a wonderful officer and we have done so much, so long, so hard together. But next month I shall join the American Staff and again we will work together.

I've enclosed the military photographs of the recent awards ceremony where Butch and I got some medals.

I'm not much in the mood to write this evening. I'm well, strong, infected eye getting better each day. Just saddened and deeply grievous of the loss of John.

My love, my sweets.

Me too.

Always,

Your Don

8 January '68
Monday Night 7:30 pm

Hi Rutchen,

Today I feel a bit better but my very insides hurt because of the sadness I feel about losing John yesterday. It was a hectic battle for "B" Troop and those wonderful brave soldiers fought their way through two NVA battalions and killed hundreds of them. Oh well, I shall never mention it again ... as he has God's blessing and to those who knew him closely, a very indelible memory.

I drove Butch up to Americal Headquarters and he left sadly, but eagerly as he is also tired from all the business we have had lately.

Received your 1 January letter. Poor Stinky, being tipsy. Ha Ha! I would have liked to have seen her. Just like her Momma, a sip or two of wine and she's gone. Great! Keep her skiing. I think that's wonderful.

I'm fine, sweetie. Tired and anxious to do something different. But okay, so don't worry.

Don't know for sure yet, but I will probably go to Hong Kong now, maybe February for my R&R, so I can buy some things. I've done a little research and you get most everything duty free whereas in the other R&R places it is more expensive and the customs are too high. I'll let you know. Is there any special wish for leather goods, shoes, bags, pearls, jade or opals? Tell me if there is because I may get some things for you that you really don't want.

It was around 3:00 am when I finally fell asleep this morning, so I'm pooped right now.

I send you so much love, need and want for you.

You too, Stinky.

Me too.

Always,

Your Don and Daddy

13 January '68

Hi Big Momma and Jacqueline,

I sit here this Saturday reading your letter from last Saturday, 6 January. How about that! I went through all the incoming mail today in hopes of a letter from you. Sure enough there was one.

Sounds like my blondies are having a good time in the snow and are real healthy from all the fresh air. That sounds like fun for both of you. Sure would like to be with you and Stinky in the snow.

I haven't really done much at all today. Did an inspection of the "Fat City" bunkers, work area and mostly some writing of awards and normal paperwork. The Colonel flew in just before lunch and I made my recommendations as to where all the officers should be assigned or switched. Some are making Captain and must get a new job, some have transferred or are in hospitals and that means we need new people.

Been trying to rest up and let the new CO. and S-3 do more so they can find out who is who and what is going on. They seem to be doing real fine.

I have been studying the price lists and shopping catalogs that Captain Conrad brought back from Hong Kong so I have an idea about $$$ and where and what things to buy. I'm looking forward to a few days rest from here and hope to get a few nice things for you, Big Momma. Also, I'll get a green uniform and a white uniform like Butch has. They are so cheap there I understand.

For goodness sakes, don't worry. I'm fine. Those medals are from way back in October and here it is well into January. I'm proud, sure, but what had to be done had to be done. It's war, honey. I don't like it ... no one does, but you have to do your job. I'm not looking or chasing for trouble. Okay? That a girl.

Things here don't seem too hopeful for any peace. Perhaps the politicians can get something done soon. I hope so for the sake of our many brave soldiers and for the welfare of these poor Vietnamese people. My infected eye is well again, and I feel fine. I'm trying to rest more and let the Colonel get his feet wet and learn.

Still haven't heard exactly what or when this staff job is supposed to be ready for me. But I imagine in another month.

Been dreaming about you, Big Momma. Oh how I want and need you!

Nothing much new to write about except that I love you, need, want miss you so so much. You too, Daddy's little Stinky

Always,

Your Don and Daddy

18 January '68
Thursday

Hi Sweetie,

Hope you miss me a little bit ... I just took a fairly warm shower outside my hooch and I got to thinking ... wouldn't it be great to take you in my shower. Yummmmmm! I had to douse myself in cold water ... but even that didn't help. I still need, want, want you so bad I can taste you. Now that is a warm thought, so warm that it makes me crazy at night thinking about you. You want me a little bit sometimes too? Better change the subject before the letter gets all wet.

It's been raining like hell again and all day. Visibility was kind of bad and it wasn't until late this afternoon that I could get a helicopter to fly. Then I just visited with Col. Cousland and the S-3 for a short conference on operations in the next few days. About 6:30 pm I flew back here and for a few hours did some paperwork.

We only allow one pet animal per troop because of the disease, rabies, etc. but every day these guys pick up something new. We have so many dogs it looks like a kennel around here. Today one came in with a monkey. We have been laughing ever so hard ... I just can't make the kid get rid of it. Jacqueline would have a great time with this zoo.

We are getting in quite a few new officers and they are all real fine young troopers. I was in Division Headquarters today and had a long chat with General Young. He said, "We are waiting on this damn Lt. Col. promotion list to find out if you made the outstanding zone so that we can give you the Lt. Col's job as a G-4 or if not, we'll find another staff assignment that would be a good one." Boy! The Army sure is playing this one like a "Hitchcock" movie...nothing but suspense. Keep your fingers crossed, honey!

Warrant Officer Dann took this picture about an hour ago with his polaroid. I'm still waiting for the prints to come back from several rolls I have taken in the last month.

Not too much new going on ... same old thing. People are all in high spirits and the squadron is working well.

Ruth circa 1958 – when Dad first saw her.

Mom's family at her wedding to Dad-Lilo, Omi, Dad, Mom, IIse, Werner and my cousins Susanne and Martina.

See no evil, Hear no evil, Speak no evil—Dad and his comrades.

*Dad and Captain Reed,
February, 1968.*

dearest
Jacqueline.
I hope these are big enough
for you to wear.
love you
Your
Daddy

Letter to me with my Christmas gift.

Veitnamese outfit he brought me in Saigon, along with the doll.

President Johnson greeting United States soldiers in Vietnam.

With President Johnson in Cam Ranh Bay December 23, 1967.

Landing on the beach in Chu Lai. August 30, 1967.

General Ryder presenting me a Bronze Star and Air Medal in February, 1968.

Dad inspecting weapons seized from the VC.

Lt. Col. Donald Carl Lundquist.

Freddy Filbert arrives to replace Dad.

Dad and Fat City sign.

Professional photo Dad asked Mom to send him in Vietnam of his Little Stinky.

The happy couple.

Fun on the beach in Norfolk shortly after Dad's Return.

Last family photo.

At Dad's grave in the 70's.

Propaganda photos from the War Museum.

Helicopter at the War Museum–the kind my father rode in daily.

A family in downtown Chu Lai.

US Air Force Base in Chu Lai.

Saigon Saigon Bar on the roof-top of the Hotel Caravelle.

Standing at the site of Dad's Fat City sign.

Indrit and me in our Vietnamese dresses.

Dick and Sam.

Ruth and Stinky (All grown up).

Me? I'm fine, sweetie. Just miss you and Stinky so, so, so much. I'll write again in the morning. For tonight, I send my love.

Me too.

Always,

Your Don and Daddy

20 January '68
Saturday night

Hi Honey!

Received your 9/10 January letter today. Glad you got the awards papers and money. Apropos money, so that you and Stinky can go on vacation I will send $400 on payday. I will have a bit over $200 for R&R, which isn't as much as I wanted to buy you lots of things. Oh well, I'll see what I can do.

Don't worry about it. I hope with the $400 you and Stinky can have a nice time too.

How is your money situation? You never did answer me after I wrote asking you about it. Does it cost more than $400 per month for you to live in Fulda or are you saving money?

I have had a busy, busy day with almost 7 hours in the helicopter today. I pulled Lt. Wheeler out of "B" Troop and combat today. In ten days he goes back to Ordinance Corps and a safe job. He has done well in the squadron winning a Silver Star, Bronze Star, Purple Heart and a Commendation Medal.

Received a letter from Capt. Dave Staley who is in the hospital in Japan. He has had another major operation, lost more weight, now feels a bit better and expects to go back to the States soon and be on some limited duty until he is completely well.

Ya! Under the 190 days to go mark now. Sure sounds better than 365, doesn't it?

I'm going to take a hot shower and get in bed. I'm dog tired from so much wind in the helicopter all day.

Don't worry now. I'll mail you the money in a few days, Big Momma.

Love, miss, need, want want you my long-legged beautiful bosomed Blonde.

Ah, I can feel the very inside of you.

Love. Me too.

Always,

Your Don and Daddy

DEPARTMENT OF THE ARMY
OFFICE OF PERSONNEL OPERATIONS
WASHINGTON, D.C. 20315

IN REPLY REFER TO

8 February 1968

Major Donald C. Lundquist
HHT, 1st Sqdn, 1st Cav
APO San Francisco 96374

Dear Major Lundquist:

Please accept my congratulations upon your selection to attend Class No. 44 of the Armed Forces Staff College.

A large group of eligible and available Armor officers were under consideration for this course, and your selection is indicative of a high standard of performance in your service to date.. I feel certain that your performance at the college will justify the selection and that the Army representatives in the class will continue the tradition of excellence established by your predecessors. Successful completion of this course will mark an important step in your career and will prepare you for a variety of challenging assignments of increasing responsibility.

Your orders to the Armed Forces Staff College will be issued in the near future with a reporting date of not later than 16 August 1968. Your assignment upon graduation from the college will be finalized about midway through the course. Please insure that we have on file prior to 1 October 1968, an up-to-date preference statement.

If you wish to take a voluntary preparatory course for officers who have been selected to attend the Armed Forces Staff College, you should write to the Chief, Nonresident Instruction, US Army Command and General Staff College, Fort Leavenworth, Kansas 66027. You must state that you are a selectee for Armed Forces Staff College and that you desire to take the Special Armed Forces Staff College Extension Course. Subject matter of the course is listed at Inclosure 1.

My best wishes for a professionally rewarding and personally enjoyable tour at Norfolk.

Sincerely,

JOHN R. BARCLAY
Colonel, Armor
Chief, Armor Branch

1 Incl

25 January '68

Dearest Ruth and Jacqueline,

YAHOO! Perhaps by now you have seen in the papers that I've been selected to attend the Armed Forces Staff College. Wunderbar!

It is a real gentleman's course. It's six months long, from August through January. It is in Norfolk, Virginia.

Great!

It's only a couple of hours by car to Washington, D.C. and our friends. I'm so excited about it and very happy. Butch Saint and I are both going together. So, Genny and you, Butch and I are once again together. I like that.

Now that means I'll leave Vietnam earlier! Happy? How much earlier I don't know but I imagine they will give me 30 to 45 days leave, about 15 days travel time, so somewhere in or around early June I should leave. Love me?

Just as soon as I can I'll find out the dates, authorized leave time, etc., I'll let you know.

Now!! Since you were rather pessimistic about the Army and my going to school and leaving Vietnam early, what do you say now, Big Momma?? WHOOPEE!

Knock on wood ... perhaps the Army will promote me on the outstanding list too. Just another few days to find out that news. I'm still hopeful, honey. Why not? Got my school, now I need the quick promotion too.

I made you a tape last night and then got smashed, I was so happy. If I had you on that beautiful love rug, you would still be on it.

How do 142 more days sound? That's about what I figure. Leaving here on or about 15 June maybe earlier if I can get 30 days leave.

I'd hug you to pieces if I had you here. I'm so happy. Give Stinky a big kiss for me and tell her Daddy will be home in June now.

I love you, Big Momma.

Me too.

Always,

Your Don and Daddy

27 January '68

Hi Big Momma,

Guess you're still rejoicing like I am about my early departure from Vietnam. Yahoo!

Today was a good day! Flew 6 1/2 hours in a new type helicopter and got credit for some kills and captured some weapons too. In for another medal.

R&R in a couple of days.

School soon ... now just promote me, Army!

Received Christmas pictures today. Wonderful. You and Jacqueline look great. She looks so happy with her new bicycle. Ha! Jacqueline's hair looks so pretty. She is a ham, posing for the pictures. Stinky, I love you.

Now I'm not so tired anymore. This new Colonel works some too and that helps me a lot. My eye is real fine ... all better.

I'm looking forward to rest, good food and a cool martini in Hong Kong. Deserve it, I think.

All the Generals told Col. Causland today that soon they are taking me up to Division as they have heard nothing but praise and expert work. Great, I'm ready for a change.

Have no worries, Big Momma. My hero days are over and I am just so happy to be leaving here earlier and back to you, even though we may only be living in Norfolk for 6 months in another apartment or even a tent.

I'M HAPPY HAPPY HAPPY!

Got a letter from Freddie Filbert today. He departs for San Francisco 30 April '68 for Vietnam and arrives is Saigon on 2 May '68 for a G-1 (Adjutants) job. Hope he stays there and doesn't try to come to field combat. But knowing my "brother" I'm sure he will try! He says Dianne is taking it well, but in true Cavalry Officer style only for face value like every woman who loves her man. Good Lord, I thought he would have more sense ... just because I am dumb. I wrote him right away tonight and told him stay, stay, stay in the staff assignment in Saigon.

Honey, don't you worry about your Big Daddy. He thinks constantly about you and our Stinky. I'm careful and a good boy. Thanks again for the great pictures. I love them, and you too, wife of a major (soon Lt. Col.) who has been selected for the top school possible before the Army War College. Proud of you too, brave Big Momma.

Love every inch of you. And I will show you on that love rug in 120 days. Hoo!

Me too.

Love you both.

Always,

Your Don and Daddy

28 January '68

Dearest Ruth,

I don't know when in 21 years in the Army one week has been so great for me.

I MADE THE "OUTSTANDING LIST FOR LIEUTENANT COLONEL" AND I LOVE YOU!!

These last five years that I have worked so hard, so long and so often ignoring you for the sake of the Army had one purpose for me ... to make something of myself quicker and faster for us. For your infinite patience, understanding, help, charm, beauty and being a dutiful Army wife, I thank you ... for you helped achieve this for me.

The rapid promotion will happen around November this year and it will be a most wonderful Birthday/Christmas present.

I'm very humble, Ruth, and I can only say that unlike you, I do have deep faith in the Army system. Yes, hard as it seems at times to be, this is the Year of the Tiger for me. Butch has made the outstanding list also, so we all should have the most happy, happy school the four of us and the children could ever have.

Are you happy, babe? I think so.

This is also the most important 5% promotion in that all doors for future assignment open very quickly and the "Bird Colonel's" list is extremely possible in 3 years, and perhaps the "Star" of a Brigadier General.

I know, Big Momma ... slow down ... not so fast. Ya! Ya! Just thinking out loud and planning our future, babe.

Just to recap this one great week:
1. Armed Forces Staff College selection
2. In for a "Silver Star"
3. Another "Bronze Star" approved
4. "Air Medal for Heroism" approved
5. "Air Medal 3rd Oak Leaf Cluster" approved
6. In for yet another valor award from a couple of days ago
7. Got my R&R approved

8. And now "Outstanding Lieutenant Colonel"
9. And you love, need and want me. Could I be happier? Hell No!
10. And I come home about 45 days earlier.
YAHOO!!! I love you.

I don't know what more good news could happen.

I believe that hard work, truth as I see it and tell it, just never can hurt you in the service. This week has proven my point beyond a shadow of a doubt.

I'm too elated to think about much else this evening other than our good fortune, my pride in you, Mrs. Lt. Col. Lundquist, and the humble satisfaction and pride I feel.

Tell Jacqueline her Daddy loves her so, so much. Your Don is one very happy husband. Be happy, too, darling. Me too.

Always,

Your Don and Daddy

1 February '68
11:00 am

Dearest Ruth and Jacqueline,

All is well, Big Momma. The last three days were something else as the NVA and VC tried very desperately to create unstable politics by terrorist tactics, mortar and artillery fire, ground attacks and attempts to whip up the villagers by capturing or assassinating local chiefs. From the south in Saigon to the northernmost borders, they went crazy and paid a very heavy price in the numbers of soldiers they lost.

Our squadron has killed several hundred enemy in the last three days and we are all fine, honey.

In a couple of hours I'm going into Chu Lai and will stay overnight with Butch. Some time tomorrow I will fly to Da Nang, spend the night there, and then leave the morning of 3 February for Hong Kong.

I was paid $156 yesterday and will not pay any bills until I return and get a full paycheck on 29 February. No sweat, I will explain to the bank. It's okay with them.

I really don't know what one can purchase in Hong Kong and what the problems of customs duty are. So anything I buy for you I shall ship to Rosie in Washington to save on the postage, duty charges, and weight allowances flying back from Germany, which will be a problem, I'm sure.

The nights are still cool enough to sleep, but the daytime is getting extremely hot again. In two minutes you're soaking wet, dripping and dust gets in every pore of your skin. I shall soak in a bath in Hong Kong. Probably, the water will be black even after several changes of water.

How are you and Jacqueline? And Mutti? Getting ready for your ski vacation? Wonderful! Please do have a good time and be careful. I hear Davos and St. Moritz were snowed in very bad and there were several avalanches in Switzerland. Sure do wish I could be with you in the sun and snow.

Please let everyone know how I appreciated their many Christmas cards, gifts, etc. I haven't had time to write and send to them all a thank you.

Well, I'm sure by now you are as happy as I am for all our good fortune of school, promotion and things. Great isn't it, Big Momma? For now I'll close and hope the telephone connections from Hong Kong to Fulda work, for that would make me ever so happy to talk to you and Stinky.

I love, love, love you and miss you dearly.

Me too.

Always,

Your Don and Daddy

3 February '68
Saturday
The President Hotel
Hong Kong

My Dearest Ruth,

All is well. I am here in Hong Kong until 8 February. Talking to you was wonderful. I am very sad to hear Mutti is in the hospital. Please give her my wishes. Sorry Jacqueline wasn't there to say hello to her Daddy. Do take your ski vacation if you can. It would be a welcome change for you. You can't spend every minute in the hospital or taking care of your mom.

Don't you worry, I'm fine and in Vietnam they are trying to make one last push before peace negotiations and I think it will all stop soon. They can't lose men like that every day.

All the stores are closed until Monday and then I shall do some shopping. Don't know prices yet, but I should be able to get you some fancy material for cocktail dresses. I really want to buy you something extra special.

For tonight I shall close. I'm going to eat the biggest steak, drink the coldest beer and have the coldest martini and, I believe, get pleasantly smashed. Butch is with me so it will be a little fun for me to laugh and relax for the first time in six months.

Again, I'm the happiest guy in the whole world because I talked to you. I love, love, love and need and want you, my Big Momma.

My special love to you.

Me too.

Always,

Your Don and Big Daddy

February 5 '68
The President Hotel
Hong Kong

My Big Momma,

You would go crazy in Hong Kong! No tax on anything and prices are amazingly cheap. So that you can make many cocktail dresses, gowns, etc., I bought you $258 worth of the most beautiful brocades, silks, beaded and sequined material and tops, and suit material. I'm proud of how beautiful you will look in them.

Butch and I have been in so many shops trying to find you and Genny beautiful things. If I had more money I would lose my head. I would like to buy you diamonds, furs, leather goods, home furniture, wigs, gold jewelry....

For me? I am having a tailor make 3 suits, 1 sport's jacket in black cashmere vicuna, 2 pairs of slacks, 1 white uniform (like Butch's), 1 lightweight summer uniform and I am having 4 pairs of shoes made for me. Cost? $250 for clothes. $40 for shoes.

If I remember correctly you have materials for 4 silk dresses; 1 silk suit; 3 beaded beautiful cocktail dresses; 1 white, 2 black and 3 full length gowns of brocade; 2 brocade and 2 voile jackets; 2 suits of wool in blue and beige; and 3 beaded cocktail jackets. That's enough to keep you sewing for a year and another baby.

I have been eating steaks, Chinese food, relaxing and even took a sauna and steam bath.

Someday we will come here together and you will be totally amazed at the things to buy. It's amazing.

For now, I'll close this short note. We are going to get some chow.

I love, need and want you, my Big Momma.

Me too.

Always,

Your Don and Daddy

7 February '68
10:00 pm
The President Hotel
Hong Kong

Hi Sweetie,

Again it was wonderful talking to you. I did not have such a good connection for when you talked I heard a lot of beep-beeps but I could still hear you.

Today I was running from one shop to the other trying to pick up the packages, gifts and things; get them wrapped; and then take a taxi, a ferry and another taxi to the US Navy Post Office. It was rush, rush, rush all day.

I did get you a medium dark brown alligator purse, key chain, cigarette case and wallet for $88. I am also having a pretty Princess Ring with sapphires and pearls and a gold bracelet and gold Chinese coin made for you. These I will send later.

My suits, uniforms and sports jacket came out beautiful. Also the 4 pairs of tailor-made shoes fit perfectly. I am very happy with all I purchased but broke and will be for the next couple of months till I pay for it all. But ... Hong Kong is a shopper's paradise. You would go wild.

The hotel will get us up at 5:30 am to get a bus to the airport, then a Pan Am flight to Da Nang, another flight to Chu Lai and I expect a new staff job waiting for me. About 130-132 days and I'll be on my way to your arms, Big Momma. I love and need and want you so, so much.

Kisses for Jacqueline from her Daddy.

For now, goodnight my sweetie.

And I love you.

Me too.

Always,

Your Don and Daddy

9 February '68
10:00 AM

Hi Sweetie,

Just woke up a bit ago. I was kind of tired last night when I got into Chu Lai and then rode by jeep to "Fat City." I took a shower and although my intentions were good, I fell asleep without writing a note.

Had all kinds of letters and cards from everyone wishing us congratulations on the promotion list, school, etc.

Also had a long letter from Colonel H explaining why he got his tail chewed out by his boss for trying to steal Butch and me for a Saigon job. He said my friend General Young called down there raising holy hell for trying to steal American Division's best two Majors. So I imagine that I will be going to American staff soon. When and what, I'll let you know as soon as I do.

The R&R trip to Hong Kong was expensive but pleasant. I hope you will like all the material I bought for you and that they arrive safely. You should receive them in about 10 days. The calls to you cost $33 each but they were worth every penny just to hear you, sweetie.

I still have some shoes, 1 jacket, a uniform and some jewelry to send you. This I will do on 1 March.

All is well here and during my absence no major actions or incidents took place. I would hope that all of the things you see on tv and read or hear will soon lead to some real peace negotiations. Time will tell. I think it will be soon.

Many, many new soldiers and officers are in the squadron due to changing jobs, etc., but they are doing quite well.

To me, the importance of this school, promotion and all my good fortune has made my many years of extra hard work so worthwhile. I am very proud and especially for you because my "lady" has the pride too. It is just marvelous, Ruth. I'm sorry Stinky was not there both times I called, but you tell her Daddy is okay and loves her very much.

The weather in Hong Kong was so cold I froze most of the time.

Although it is rainy and cool here, it is much warmer than in Hong Kong and it feels good in comparison.

My driver just brought me a cup of hot coffee. Ahhh. So good ... would prefer yours, of course, but that will be soon, Big Momma. So many good things you have which I want. Mmmmmmmm! and they all taste and feel so good.

How is Mutti doing, Ruth? Don't you worry you can tell me what's going on with her. I see enough here to make ones hair turn white and I want you to keep me informed about her. Please do tell her that I miss her too and hope she gets well real, real soon.

Special hugs and kisses for you and our Jacqueline. Love, miss and need you. Me too.

Always,

Your Don and Daddy

P.S. Only four more months and I'll be home.

16 February '68
Friday Morning

Hi Sweetie,

Since I've been back things are busy and time is flying by. Been trying to catch up on some paperwork, special projects and loose ends from just one week's absence.

Today retired 4-Star General Clarke and the vice commander here in Vietnam 4-Star General Abrahams, plus our C.G. Major General Koster visited us today to find out our current situation. They were pleased and congratulated us for our 28 to 1 kill ration. In other words, we have killed 28 more times or 700 VC to the 25 soldiers we have lost. That is the highest and least in all of Vietnam.

Then General Ryder, the assistant Division Commander came in for an awards ceremony, and to my surprise, pinned my second cluster to my Air Medal and a 3rd Cluster for Heroism on 27 January. I learned yesterday that a 4th Cluster for Heroism will be presented for actions way back last September and another Bronze Star for last Nov-Dec for Meritorious Achievement. I'll send you the orders, certificates and medals when I've got them all together this week.

Fred wrote a long letter and he most definitely wants my job in the field when he arrives on 2-3 May. He knows what he is doing, has Dianne's full blessing, has written Col. H and has a good chance of getting my job. It will be good for Fred, as my job is a busy one and a safe one where he can learn much. I'll keep you posted if he succeeds.

Just reread the last three letters you sent and guess I didn't answer all of your questions.

#1 - You look beautiful in your short fur coat. I like it very much. Particularly the big blonde under it. That's where I would like to be...under it, over it and around it.

#2 - Our littlle ski-bunny is just as beautiful as her mother. I'm proud of you both.

#3 - Yes, I remember 9 years ago skiing on the Wasserkuppe with you. Lots of fun following your beautiful bottom down the ski trail.

As it stands now, and I won't know exactly until early May, it has been adjusted that I must leave here by 1 July. Since I have applied for permission to go through Germany to have a few days leave and pick you both up en route to the USA, it's possible that I could leave here as early as 1 June. I'll know exactly later. Just be patient, Big Momma. The Army has been very good to us this year and they will continue to do so. Leaving here one or two months early should make you very happy ... me too. So there! Give me a big kiss and smile also. Okay! That's better. Now keep smiling. I like your dreams with me in your arms, they make me tingle all over, too. Don't you worry, that day will come soon. Just four more months and if I'm lucky, only 3 1/2. So smile!

Yes, I dream about a comfortable home with all our things together again. Even though it's only for 6-7 months in Norfolk, Virginia and then someplace else again ... it doesn't make any difference where we are. As long as we are together, I'm happy.

I talked to Armor Branch and they say, "Lieutenant Colonel's DO NOT get second tours of duty in Vietnam." There! Does that make you happy? Yes? Okay.

Glad you are proud of your Big Daddy. I am happy and proud of you and for you, Colonel's Lady!

I'll close tonight. It is now 10:20 pm and I must clean up some things and get some sleep, for I have a busy schedule in the morning.

I love you, Big Momma. You, too, Stinky.

Me too.

Always,

Your Don and Daddy

17 February '68
10:00 pm Saturday night

Hi Big Momma,

All is well. I've been over at the Lt. Capt.'s hooch for the last hour having a drink to celebrate Lt. Davis's promotion to Captain today. Plus, we received 5 new officers in the squadron in the last two days and I have shifted and moved many officers around to give them new experiences and jobs, so there was an hour of festive happiness. Capt. Prothers just returned from R&R to Hawaii and he had a ball with Kathy and sadly is back in the squadron.

I have enclosed a shoulder patch from our attached Air Cavalry Troop "C" 7/17 and the name makes me laugh so hard. You ... my Ruth .... I don't have you here so I'm "Ruthless." And you know the toast I always give, "To the Ladies and Horses of Cavalry and to the men who ride them." I, being the "Rider." So don't you think it is a beautiful patch so appropriate for me..." Ruthless Riders."

On Valentine's Day, for my love for you, I ran an operation on 14 February called "Operation Ruthless," moving along route "Lonesome" and took objective "Rider." It was extremely successful and with Dave Roessler's Troop and some South Vietnamese Rangers we killed 39 VC and captured 9 more. It was beautiful and every one I run till June will be known as Ruthless Rider I, II, III, IV, etc.

Been looking through all the pictures you have sent me. Jacqueline is getting so big. She's still a real strong built child and, golly, I miss my Stinky so much. She is such a pretty girl ... like her beautiful mother.

All is quiet here and everyone is doing well lately.

I hope some of the packages I mailed from Hong Kong start to arrive soon. You will have enough material to sew and make the most beautiful gowns, dresses and suits for a good while.

Yes, Big Momma! I can almost feel the kisses you send me. Oh, how I miss you.

After receiving the Lt. Col. promotion list, I imagine the last week of October or the 1st week of November I'll be promoted. Great Birthday and Xmas holiday season a coming. Oh! I'm so happy. Goodnight, my sweeties. I dearly love and miss you both. Love you.

Always,

Your Don and Daddy

21 February '68
Jacqueline's 4th Birthday

Dearest Stinky,

Daddy is well and am very happy for my "Four Year Old Little Girl." I sent you a birthday card and birthday tape early so to be sure it would arrive for you on this day.

I am so proud of you, Jacqueline, and I hope you know how much your Daddy loves and misses you.

Soon we shall have fun together and we will swim, play, read, laugh and sing together "Happy Birthday to you, my sweetheart."

The biggest hug and kiss for you. I miss and love you.

Ruth,

Received your 12 February letter today and I do so hope that Mutti is well enough that you are now in the sunshine and snow of Arosa.

Today I wrote a letter to Mrs. Long. I expressed our sympathy and told her of the many times I had seen, talked with, ate lunch with and worked with Jack. Yes, it was very sad. He was an Infantry soldier, a good one and a brave one.

Looks fairly certain that Fred will get my job when he arrives in early May.

All is well, honey. Don't worry. I'm fine, strong, healthy and happy that the days are passing quickly. We are close to that 120 day mark now.

Daddy loves you, Stinky, and Happy, Happy Birthday.

Love and miss you so.

Me too.

Always,

Your Don and Daddy

25 February '68
10:00 pm Sunday night

My Dearest Ruth and Jacqueline,

How are my blondies this evening? I'm so sorry you couldn't go on the ski vacation as I know how much you were looking forward to it. Perhaps you can go in March or even early April. I hope so. If not, why not go someplace in Germany for a few days. Perhaps to Garmisch with Ilse and Werner, just some place for a breather.

After several days, I got your 17 February letter today. Ya! I'll bet Stinky was all excited about her birthday. Wish I were there.

Don't worry about what is on the Custom's tags. I rushed so much to get to the Hong Kong Post Office filling out so many tags, I forgot what was in each box. Hope all arrives okay. Everything was insured for at least $50. That is the maximum free customs I could mail, the contents cost a hell of a lot more, but I couldn't pay taxes too. You should receive the things I mailed from here in the next 10-12 days. Did you like the suits I had made?

Oh! Our Jacqueline is getting bigger every day. Fine, I'm happy she is so tall.

Got letters from Fred today telling me he is so excited about getting my job. It's all set with all the headquarters in Saigon, Americal Division and here, of course. I'm happy for him because he is a good man and he must prove himself. But I told him in no uncertain terms of his responsibilities to Dianne, the children, etc. Unlike me, he has no reason to charge around. He will make the Lt. Col.'s list within the next year. So, he should take it easy and not be like I was.

I also told him I'm taking it easy once he gets here. I'm so happy for Fred ... he didn't want a Saigon job ... he is Cavalry and this squadron does things correctly, superbly and right. He will be proud to serve in this unit as I have been. We can share this as men.

It's late and I want to finish a book I started called "Topaz" about the Cuban Missile Crisis. It's great.

I love you, want you, need you so much. I keep having the wildest dreams about our love rug and just relaxed happiness, laughs, candlelit dinners, dancing, Cognac, games, friends, Stinky, fun, happiness. Damn this hellhole of a place.

I want, miss and need you both so much.

Always,

Your Don and Daddy

DEPARTMENT OF THE ARMY
HEADQUARTERS AMERICAL DIVISION
APO San Francisco 96374

GENERAL ORDERS   9 February 1968
NUMBER   584

AWARD OF THE AIR MEDAL
(THIRD OAK LEAF CLUSTER)

1. TC 320. The following AWARD is announced.

LUNDQUIST, DONALD C. 097939, MAJOR, ARMOR, United
States Army, Headquarters and Headquarters Troop, 1st Squadron, 1st
Cavalry APO 96374
    Awarded: Air Medal with "V" Device (3d Oak Leaf Cluster)
    Date action: 27 January 1968
    Theater: Republic of Vietnam
    Reason: For heroism while participating in aerial flight. Major
        Lundquist distinguished himself by heroic action on 27 Jan-
        uary 1968 while serving as the executive officer for the 1st
        Squadron, 1st Cavalry. On that date, Major Lundquist was
        participating in an orientation flight in a light observa-
        tion flight helicopter when the aircraft suddenly came
        under intense ground fire. Immediately, Major Lundquist
        reported the action and due to the delay in getting a
        cavalry platoon in the area, he remained in the area plac-
        ing constant suppressive fire on the enemy. When the door
        gunner's machinegun jammed, Major Lundquist quickly pre-
        pared the gun on his side of the helicopter and directed
        the aircraft into position to enable him to engage the
        enemy. With his accurate suppressive fire, Major Lundquist
        personally killed one and wounded two of the enemy. While
        his aircraft was still at a dangerously low level and subject
        to enemy fire, Major Lundquist directed the cavalry platoon
        into the action. Major Lundquist's heroic actions and devo-
        tion to duty are in keeping with the highest traditions of
        the military service and reflect great credit upon himself,
        the Americal Division, and the United States Army.
    Authority: By direction of the President under the provisions of
        Executive Order 9158, 11 May 1942, as amended by Execu-
        tive Order 9242-A, 11 September 1942.

FOR THE COMMANDER:

OFFICIAL: NEIS A. PARSON JR.
                                             Colonel, GS
                                             Chief of Staff

DONALD Y. B. CHUNG
LTC, AGC
Adjutant General

DEPARTMENT OF THE ARMY
HEADQUARTERS AMERICAL DIVISION
APO San Francisco 96374

GENERAL ORDERS   20 March 1968
NUMBER   1449

AWARD OF THE SILVER STAR

1. TC 320. The following AWARD is announced.

LUNDQUIST, DONALD C. 097939, MAJOR, ARMOR, United
States Army, Headquarters and Headquarters Troop, 1st Squadron, 1st
Cavalry APO 96374
Awarded: Silver Star
Date action: 27 and 28 February 1968
Theater: Republic of Vietnam
Reason: For gallantry in action against a hostile force on 27 and 28
          February 1968 in the Republic of Vietnam. Major Lundquist
          distinguished himself by intrepid actions while serving as the
          task force commander of combined air cavalry and armored
          cavalry elements on a search and destroy mission of Tam
          Ky. His actions as the task force commander were marked by
          his determined and aggressive spirit, and his professional
          competence in coordinating the efforts of the two elements.
          Throughout the two days, Major Lundquist remained in the
          very center of the heaviest fighting, which was directed at
          two main force battalions of enemy soldiers entrenched in
          well-fortified positions. In addition to his superb control
          of the situation, he personally engaged the enemy forces on
          several occasions. With grim and calm determination, he con-
          stantly placed himself at the very point of the heaviest enemy
          automatic weapons and rocket fire. The two day operation was
          marked by two distinct types of engagements, which included
          knifing into enemy fortified positions, and pursuit of fleeing
          enemy forces. Major Lundquist performed both tasks with
          aggressiveness and courage, which served to inspire his troops.
          The entire operation accounted for 180 enemy killed, and
          Major Lundquist was personally credited with killing 11 enemy
          soldiers. Major Lundquist's unquestionable valor in close
          combat against a numerically superior hostile force is in
          keeping with the highest traditions of the military service
          and reflects great credit upon himself, the Americal Division,
          and the United States Army.
Authority: By direction of the President under the provisions of the
            Act of Congress, approved 9 July 1918.

29 February '68

My Dearest Ruth and Jacqueline,

Several very busy days have passed and I have not had time to write. All is well. I'm safe, sound and gloriously happy at the successes of the last few days.

While flying North to visit Col. Causland, I spotted about 300 VC in open fields running and moving towards Tam Ky about 30 km north of here. For the next 11 hours it was the battle a commander dreams of. I called in four Cavalry Platoons and all the helicopters I could get and we killed 180 VC, took 18 prisoners, captured over 150 weapons, rock mortars and piles of equipment. I personally killed 11 myself and was given much credit for the whole show. Almost every General around came to congratulate Col. Causland and me.

My adrenaline is starting to come back to normal now. I have never seen such fantastic luck and violent reaction by our people. They were wonderful. In all the action only four men in our squadron were slightly wounded. Just scratches, and none require any hospitalization. Yes, sweetie. I got a couple of scratches on my left leg below the knee. No, no! It's just like when you run into the corner of the bed and bruise your leg. Nothing more!

So, I'll get another Purple Heart. Also, Col. Causland has submitted a recommendation for a Silver Star for Heroism.

Ya! Ya! I know what you are saying, but to kill VC is my business and there is no where here I would rather be than with this squadron around me. They are great! I say it was a battle a commander can only dream of as the enemy was completely beaten and now has packed up its few survivors and headed for the mountains.

This all happened from about 12:30 pm on the 27th and yesterday from 9am-4pm. I slept like a baby last night I was just so tired and emotionally spent.

After a good night's sleep I am now somewhat relaxed and feel good and happy as hell. Knowing you, your answer is "My dear, dear Don!" Yes, Ruth, but never forget if you think I chase these things, you are wrong.

They just happen in Vietman and you can't run away and ignore the enemy. It would be crazy.

I am very grateful and proud of the fact that no man in this squadron was hurt and that so many VC were killed and beaten.

I'm fine, Ruth. I look at the calendar and realize we have only a short number of days to wait, Big Momma.

Love Always,

Your Don and Daddy

3 March '68
10:00 pm

Dearest Ruth,

All is well. I just returned to "Fat City" a bit ago after spending the day at our other location in celebration of the squadron's 135th birthday. It rained during the whole awards ceremony but just everyone was there and I was so proud of our men. The Generals all had great praise for us. After the US awards were presented, a Vietnamese General pinned the highest Viet decorations on seventeen of us. Col. C, myself, Butch, Saint, Capt. Roessler and a few enlisted men. I am quite proud of this one.

After the ceremony we had Cavalry Punch and food and toasts and laughs and a few hours of drinking. It was just great and all full of wit and laughs. Later when the pictures come back I'll send them, sweetie.

I was really hurting for money to send you this month as I had double car payments and double bills because of R&R. But in typical fashion, I was invited to play poker last night and only had $20 and this morning I have $450. I have enclosed $350 to you. We are all caught up now. How is that for luck? Great!!

I'm glad Stinky had a great birthday and was happy.

Also glad you liked the things I sent you. Makes me happy, since the many dollars mean nothing unless you like the things you got.

Big Momma, I'm so happy the days are really rushing by and I love, need and want you so much it hurts.

It will be such great fun all being together again. I can only think how many laughs, love and just great things to do to each other, for each other and for our Stinky too.

I'll write more in the evening or tomorrow. In a few days the newspapers will have a big cover story about the squadron. I'll make every effort to get copies.

I love you, my Ruth.

You too, Stinky.

Me too.

Always,

Your Don and Daddy

6 March '68

Hi Big Momma,

Just a short note. All is well ... I'm fine. And you my, Sweetie. How are you? I got your 27 February letter. You sound so sad. Yes, I know you are sick with worry and Mutti being sick makes it so hard for you.

You keep Jacqueline talking about her Daddy because in a few months we will all be so, so happy.

Checked in to Americal Headquarters and they said I'll leave around 15-20 June via Germany. I need your passport number, sweetie.

Glad you keep getting packages I've sent you. Enclosed are some pictures from 2 January and mid-February at the awards function. Hope you like them.

Last night, although sleepy, the guys came to my place to play poker and, as usual, I won. About $425! So.... I did what I've wanted to for a long time and today I bought you a very beautiful diamond engagement ring for $225 plus another gold dinner ring that wasn't expensive but pretty. I got size 6½ because to special order your exact size takes 8 to 12 weeks. I couldn't get a matching wedding ring in gold, but can get it in about 8 weeks per the salesman at the PX in Chu Lai.

Enclosed is a ring size chart. Tell me if you want me to get it or just buy one in Germany. Whatever you want, darling. Just tell me quickly if I should order it. It's plain gold, no diamonds in the band.

Why? Because I love you so and for your Birthday and our Anniversary I wanted something extra beautiful and special for you, my big beautiful blonde darling. I'll have it mailed tomorrow.

More good news! I'll probably get promoted in early June prior to leaving here as they expect to promote this list extra fast. Isn't that great? Gets better all the time.

All is well. I'm going to read a bit now and get some sleep. I love every inch of you. Kisses for Jacqueline. Daddy loves you both so, so much.

Goodnight my sweeties. Me too.

Always,

Your Don and Daddy

15 March '68

Dear Ruth and Jacqueline,

All is well. I'm fine and as always, busier than hell. We have received a lot of new men, officers and equipment so I'm busy getting everything and everyone on their feet again.

Been a long day again. Had more Generals visiting than usual ... General Beach, the Hawaii Pacific Commander, Lt. General Palmer, the Deputy Vietnam Commander and all the division Generals, too.

After a briefing, big congratulations, pat on the head, "good work, keep charging" they left. We need fewer Generals and more sleep.

Glad you like the princess ring! How about the gold bracelet and gold coins? Wait till your birthday present ring arrives. That is the nice one and the expensive one for my Big Momma.

I'll send you a couple more medals when they give them to me soon. A "Silver Star" for actions on 27-28 February and another "Purple Heart" for 26 February. Getting so many of the damn things. I keep saying I have enough and I do. Your "surprise" sounds like a nice case to put them in. Am I right?

No, Fred is not crazy. My job is a good one. He is a man, a soldier and a darn good officer. Of any Major I know, Fred will do a good job and it is very important that he does.

Things have quieted down a lot and everyone is catching their breath a little. We have all been working very hard and very successfully.

Tell Stinky I look forward to getting her Easter painting.

Give everyone my love. Thanks to Lilo and Ernst for their letter.

For now, sweetie, I love you both so much.

Me too.

Always,

Your Don and Daddy

16 March '68
Saturday Evening
17 March '68
Sunday Morning

Hi Big Momma,

I just started this letter with the date and then took a shower, lay down on my bed and never woke up until this morning - Sunday. Guess I was just bone tired and needed the sleep.

All is well. I'm fine. With the troops real busy, sometimes my days run into nights and then to day again before I sleep, but that's no problem. Time goes by much faster that way. I can hardly believe it is the 17th already. Great! Only about 90 days left now.

Today at 11:30 the Vice Commander of the Pacific Command, a Lt. General, arrives for a briefing and then at 1:30 General Young, my buddy, arrives to present some awards to our men. Then from 16:30 to 18:00 we plan to have all the officers together for a briefing and a cold St. Patrick's Day beer.

I'm getting more excited as the days roll by to be on my way to you and Jacqueline. These past almost eight months have been sometimes hard and frustrating, glorious, sad, lonely, unhappy, happy in thankful prayer and unlike Korea ... a totally different experience for me. I'll leave here proudly and happy that I have done my part and then some.

Mom and Pop Filbert haven't written me in a long time. Guess they are quite concerned about Fred, but he will do well here and they should not worry.

How are you coming on our love rug?

For now my sweeties, I send my love to both of you.

Love and need you.

Me too.

Always,

Your Don and Daddy

21 March '68
Thursday 10:35 pm

Sweetie,

I've been busier than hell the last couple of days and haven't had time to write. All is well. I'm fine, just busy.

Mail has been slow from you but today I feel good because I received your letters dated 14 &15 March.

You hero is fine! Just getting tired of all the blood, guts and war here. We are doing so well that it's more trouble briefing Generals on what and how we do things than winning great battles. Yesterday we got another tremendous battle won. Capt. Dave Roessler was magnificent, as usual.

Yes, I'm lucky in poker (and everything else, too)! Can't help it if I keep winning ... it's great.

Oh! Your diamond ring arrived. I'm happy you like it. Now that we are "engaged", I'll have to sleep with you in June to see if you really fit well. Won't it be fun trying? Ya......hoo! I'm ready.

What will you do when I get home? Don't worry I'll only sleep when we can't go anymore each night.

I'm happy you like your ring and I need you, my woman. My Ruth.

Tomorrow there is another General's visit. Lt. General Kinnard is coming from Washington. Ah! It's like a travel bureau at times.

Give Stinky her Daddy's love and an extra special kiss. Daddy loves her so much.

That's right ... don't move. As I lift off your blouse, undo your bra, ahhh, those breasts ... kiss each nipple ... ease down your nylons, lie down, slide off those panties and ohhh! just kiss you a while ... now I've got you deeper, deeper...! can hear you moaning now ... kissing each other.

Had enough? No! Okay, in eighty some days, I'll ask you again. Now that I can't sleep, hope you can't either. Love, need, want, miss you, my love. Me too. Always,

Don and Daddy

P.S. I know, I know. I'm a naughty boy, but I think you love it and me!

P.P.S. I've enclosed a letter from Fred so you can see how excited he is about coming here.

15 March '68
Friday

Dear Don,

I really appreciate everything you've done to get me your job. I'm quivering with anticipation and can't wait to get there.

I've been very busy briefing my replacement, getting "honored" as you can see in the paper, three going away parties this weekend, last minute bill paying, arrangements for cutting off the gas, etc., and all sorts of last minute things that pile up.

Monday and Tuesday the packers get to work; Wednesday house cleaning and 07:20 Thursday off in the big bird to Philadelphia. Marion will meet us at the Aerodrome then off to Auburn to visit my parents for a week. On to San Francisco on 28 March to find a house, move in, etc. Port Call NLT 0100 hors on 30 April. Should see you on 2 or 3 May!

Had an Americal Welcome from the G-1 with a copy of its achievements. I'm anxious to see you, bro. You are really great!

Love,

Fred, Dianne, Fred Jr., Tim and Joanna

24 March '68
Sunday Evening

Hi Sweetie!

Got your acknowledgement card on the ring size and Passport #.
Great! Now I'll order the matching wedding band. Hell! I might as well
marry you now that I know your ring size from memory. Got to see if I
remember the other sizes of you, too.

All is well. Had a busy day and from 5-6 pm got all our officers
together for a couple of beers and dinner. It was great. We relaxed for an
hour or so.

Enclosed is the "Silver Star" orders from the day I killed a bunch in
February. It's the USA's 3rd highest award for heroism and I'm proud of
this one more than all the rest I've received. They will probably present it
next Sunday afternoon at which time I'll mail the Certificate and the
Medal. Ya! Ya! I've quit all this hero stuff, I promise.

Love you and need you, my Darling.

Kisses for Stinky.

Love.

Me too.

Always,

Your Don and Daddy

26 March '68
Tuesday Night

Hi Big Momma,

Now it is 27 March. Started this letter last night, but was too tired.

All is well. I'm fine and have been busy moving our logistics base and administrative sections to two new locations. It took several days to move all the darn stuff we have here. I moved north a little and everyone from old "Fat City" is now together with the rest of the squadron on one hill.

I'm living in a well built bunker almost 8 feet under ground with an ice box, lights, an easy chair, water cooler, wall locker for clothes, desk and grass rugs on the floor, so it is a comfortable place to come back to each evening. It's cooler, too.

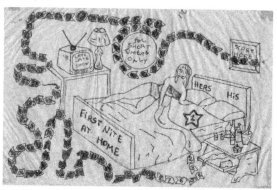

Finally got your letters. Thanks for the drawings and notes from Stinky.

I got a brochure explaining school in Norfolk, Virginia, and all about the housing, etc. Seems we can get a two bedroom, living room, kitchen, bath, porch for $92.50 on post for students. It's substandard housing, but for the five months we will be there, it will do. I'm going to file for it now, soon as I talk to Butch about his plans.

I've got to run. I have a staff and CO. meeting in about 15 minutes. I'll write more later, sweetie. Love you so much. Be good, Stinky.

Daddy misses you both.

Me too.

Always,

Your Don and Daddy

4 April '68

Hello there, Sweetie!

Is all well at home? It has now been many, many days since I heard from you in any way at all.

I'm real fine, honey. Busy with conferences, work and planning future operations, and lots of time spent flying. I like it that way because then I fall asleep quickly.

Soon it will be Easter and I wish I could hide eggs and have fun with Jacqueline.

Jelly beans, chocolate bunnies and little golden chickadees for you, my Stinky.

Enclosed are a couple more pictures.

The stupid one with the orange hat is me at the back door of our new S-4 shop in Chu Lai. I went in to inspect their operations and made this for you.

How is Mutti?

I do hope you are well.

Love and need you so, so much.

Me too.

Always,

Your Don and Daddy

6 April '68
Saturday evening
9:15 pm

Dearest Ruth,

Hope you and Stinky are up and well once more! I'm fine. All is OK. Today was a busy day as I was making sure some new armor hydraulic bridges were constructed and trying to train some operators to know how to use them properly.

Just looking at both your pictures. This is the first bunker I have had where I could put them on the wall without dust, rain and dampness ruining them. Pretty Jacqueline and my Big Momma. Ya! I miss you both.

Listening to the radio ... about the assassination of Martin Luther King. My God, what a mess at home with riots, looting, burning and the way the factions of black and white lash out at each other. The negro soldiers I have are as good and some better and braver than the others. We live and fight together and they bleed and cry the same as any brother here. A damn shame!

Tomorrow most of our troops come back in by noon from operations and at 1:00 pm we have the General coming to present two Silver Stars and 13 Bronze Stars. I enclose a military news clipping of the action for which I won my Silver Star.

Fred won't believe the inside of my bunker when I turn it over to him. I painted it clean, have an easy chair we brought from Fort Hood and with a little bit of imagination one can almost believe it's not like living in a cellar. Beats living like a rat in a hole.

Listening to some old tapes from you and Jacqueline. So homesick for you!

Get well, Big Momma.

Love, need and want you both.

Me too.

Always,

Your Don and Daddy

8 April '68

My Big Momma and Jacqueline,

Now that I've received your letters of 1 and 2 April I'm worried to pieces. I've contacted the Red Cross to find our how you, Jacqueline and Mutti are.

My dear, dear Ruth - don't get sick ... get well.

I need you for my life! Please, please God. Make you well. Oh Lord! What a situation. My tail hanging out for nine months already and the Lord watching over me and ZAP ... you guys get ill. I pray! I pray! You get well quickly.

If necessary, I'll go see the General unless I hear from the Red Cross by supper tonight.

I'm fine and well. You both must be that way too.

I love you, Ruth.

Please get well.

Love you.

Always,

Your Don and Daddy

12 April '68
Good Friday
9:00 pm

Dear Ruth and Jacqueline,

All is well. I'm fine. I heard from the Red Cross this morning that you were both getting better. I'm happy and thankful.

In two days it is Easter! I am nowhere near any place to buy Easter cards for you or anyone in the family. So, do wish just everyone ... family, friends, neighbors, many greeting from me.

Of course you both know my Special Wishes are for you. I will be thinking about you so much.

We are very busy and the troops are doing just wonderfully.

Ya! Ya! I'll be so happy to see you again. And your poor mother. Please, please give her all my love and tell her my thoughts are with her.

I try to wear myself out each day in order to sleep well at night. I am so lonely for you and Jacqueline. All the other things of material value like hot showers, clean clothing, food and drink mean little to me. It is you I miss and love and need.

Pretty soon it is your Birthday. Then we zoom right through the month of May and before you know it ... there we all are jumping up and down at the passenger terminal in Frankfurt. Oh! The thought of it sounds so great. Patience, Big Momma, and our day will come.

I've got a little work to do yet, so I'll close for the evening.

Love and miss my darlings.

Happy Easter.

Me too.

Always,

Your Don and Daddy

14 April '68
Easter Sunday

Dearest Ruth and Jacqueline,

Another Sunday without you, my darling.

Surprisingly, I'm happy almost to the point of tears, for today the squadron and particularly "A" Troop led by Capt. Dave Roessler, accomplished the impossible combat mission.

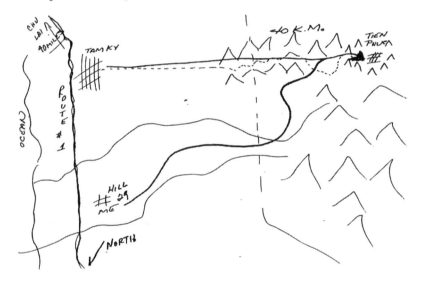

For nine days we have fought some bitter battles opening a road, building bridges and killing the enemy of a village of 18,000 Vietnamese who have been surrounded by the VC and NVA for four years. It was such a hard week for Dave and his men. The difficulties of enemy, terrain and jungles were fierce, but today at 4:00 pm we broke through to the thousands of children and families who were crying with happiness. It was a good Easter.

Me? All week I spent six to ten hours a day in a helicopter with Col. Causland firing machine guns at VC. We killed a bunch, somewhere around 45 and I managed again to get some pieces of stuff in my right wrist, mostly powder burns and metal fragments from machine gun fire.

But the satisfaction of watching the victory march into that village made it all worth it. I am so proud of these guys it makes me just all loose inside.

Dave was wounded twice and still accomplished his mission. He has done well in the now almost four months he has commanded.

We had a short Easter Service for a Lieutenant and some men who were killed this week. It is truly an emotional Easter day. Tears and sadness ... yet the soldiers feel the rewards of victory in battle ... and then there were the faces of those Vietnamese people and children in the village of TienPhuoc!

I'm now sitting in my bunker again at Fat City, not Chu Lai where my S-1 and S-4 are. I just had a shower, read your letter of 7 April and counted my blessings.

I have never been worried here .... scared to hell, yes. Shot at, yes. Hit, yes .... but overall worry, no. Why? Because of you and Jacqueline. This is the "Year of the Tiger" for me and it has proved itself again and again and again and again.

The whole squadron is to receive the "State of Vietnam Presidential Unit Award ... another medal, plus two USA awards ... the Presidential Unit Citation and Valorous Unit Award. I could put in for another Purple Heart but I won't until I leave here in June. The General is putting Col. Causland and me in for some kind of medal for these last nine days. Ya! Ya! Ruth, like I keep telling you, don't worry. Your Big Daddy takes care of himself and his men ... and soon I'll be home to take care of you and Stinky.

Just crossed another day off our Short Timers calendar and I figure we have around 60-63 days yet to wait. Sure sounds great, doesn't it!

Must be getting short, I just received mail for Fred Filbert to hold until his arrival in 2 1/2weeks.Peace talks! That sounds nice, but progress and agreements are politician's work, not soldier's. Our solutions might not be favorable to the politicians.

Negro problems in America? We have none of that here. For shame at home!

Best I close this Easter Sunday letter. Love to all family and friends.
My special love to my Sweeties!
Love you.
Me Too.
Always,

Your Don and Daddy

20 April '68
Saturday Eve
9:30 pm

Dearest Ruth and Jacqueline,

Another week just zoomed by and I sit in my bunker this Saturday evening lonely and missing you both so, so much. Down in the dumps quite a bit this evening because I just need and miss you so.

Otherwise, I'm fine, healthy and doing well. We had Generals in and out all week, changes of missions and enough paperwork to keep several Majors busy.

Today, General Hollis, an ex-Colonel Brigade Commander from Kitzingen and a visitor to our squadron while we were in Texas, came from Washington and visited us. He was, of course, highly complimentary of our combat record to date and he was very warm and friendly to me. "Old buddy" stuff which went well with my boss and Generals. He said General Connor, my old C.G. from Wurzburg is critically ill in Walter Reed Hospital with recent massive heart attacks.

The mail was kind of slim this week. Got one letter from you. I know there is never much news but regardless, I need news of you both, my sweeties.

Col Causland and I were talking last night about our wives and he whisked out a picture of her - a nice looking, tall, blond, ex-Playboy bunny from the Miami Playboy Club. A divorcee with two children and now one of their own, too. He said that Glenn Petrenko was floored because he couldn't think of Causland's wife as Playboy Bunny. Ya! Ya! A glorified cocktail waitress but he is happy as hell with her and when we are all in Washington we can get together. He thinks you will like her and we can swap combat stories and enjoy some golf and tennis.

Just listened to radio news of Vietnam and the world. Here news is encouraging ... the rest of the world seems like a mad house. Rioting now in Germany over Rudy Weisitch. Who's he? Negroes! Whites! Gold! French! England! Peace Talks! Damn, what a mess.

Sorry no diamonds this month. No birthday card either, but you know my love for you is real and true. I love you, my Ruth.

Always,

Your Don and Daddy

24 April '68
Wednesday
10:00 pm

Dearest Ruthchen and Jacqueline,

Umm! Hmmmm! Mail delivery in 6 days time. That's a record. Got you letter from 18 April today. Feast or famine here with mail delivery. Got a letter from Rob Roller, Col. H and Diner's Club with a bill for purchases from Hong Kong. Wow! Oh well, no sweat!

How am I? Oh, okay. Just tired and yet on the other hand ambitious and full of energy as ever. Just moody at times. Oh, I'm healthy and fit, but discouraged at politicians' approach to peace negotiations.

Oh! Did it rain, rain, rain this day! Except for a few hours late this afternoon, flying weather was bad. Soaking wet!

Time? Yes, I guess you're right. I've been on duty and away from Jacqueline a good part of her four years. But that doesn't mean I don't love her. We'll have lots of time together.

Money? I mailed a separate note with $400 in money order in early April. Hope you received it by now.

No! Medals don't make me happy ... they make me relieved because they are all things behind me, passed, over. I wouldn't want to do them again. I have slowed down a lot, don't worry.

About some 50 days now. Really great, huh? Fred should arrive in about 10 days. My, oh my! Time is passing quickly.

Holler out the window to Jacqueline in the playground that her Daddy loves her so much.

I just took a cold shower. Ummmm! I could think of some warmer showers with you. Soon, Big Momma.

A bit sleepy, so I'll close for this evening. Love you.

Me too.

Always,

Your Don and Daddy

28 April '68
Sunday

Dearest Ruth and Jacqueline,

A bonanza! Two letters from you to cheer my lonely Sunday evening.

Things were relatively quiet yesterday and today I spent the day visiting all our platoons, solving personal problems of the men, writing efficiency reports and medal recommendations. Last night I spent another lonely Saturday night thinking of you, our love rug and our Jacqueline and I was sad because I had no mail from you to cheer me up.

Ah! But tonight is different. Mail from my Big Momma from 19 and 21 April.

Ya! Ya! Big Momma. Eight years on 4 June. Eight wonderful years with the gal I love more as each year goes by. Like good cheese, we get better with age. Or is it wine? I guess both! I'll show you how good on our love rug after some wine and cheese.

Vietnam has done many things for me in realizing what is important in life. I don't think I have changed at all outside, but inside I'm bursting with desire to love you and Jacqueline so much more.

The pressure on a man here is something terrific and to keep it up seven days a week, month in and month out, is greater than I expected and ever faced in my life. It has scared me many, many times but I thank my stars I won these battles with myself and came out of them the right way each time. Oh yeah!

Fred wrote of spending a great weekend in San Francisco with Dianne. Dinner, floorshow, topless go-go show and this weekend, he and Dianne will do it again. By the time you receive this letter, Fred will be sitting next to me and learning my job. Small world at times.

Yes, Ruth! The human touch of Jacqueline wanting her arm tattooed just like her Daddy warms my heart. You tell Jacqueline her Daddy loves and misses her so much. We shall have much fun together, real soon.

Ya! Ya! Time will go fast now, only some 50 odd days. You bring that love rug to the airport in Frankfurt. Afraid? It will be soo nice and soo crazy! Ya! Hoo!It's now after 10:30 pm. I had a shower and am sleepy and shall dream of you, in you, around you, on top of you, on the bottom of you. Kiss, kiss, mmmmm!

Love you.

Me too.

Always,

Your Don and Daddy

30 April '68
Tuesday

Hi Sweetie!

HAPPY BIRTHDAY RUTH!

Birthdays come and birthdays go
But on this one you should know
I miss you much, I miss you true,
And I give all my love to you.

Though many miles distance we are away
I hope you feel, on this special day
That I'm thinking of you and I sing
Birthday wishes and the Diamond ring.

Love you. Always. Me too. Your Don

All is well. I'm fine and just miss you and Jacqueline so much.

Rained like hell yesterday night and until this morning. Feel like a bullfrog in early spring ... I'm soaking wet and horny too.

Relatively quiet today. Our helicopters were busy but the ground troops were resting some.

The Colonel and Major Medberry both have recommended me for an Army Commendation Medal for Heroism for way back on 28 March and 13-14 April when I killed a few more. No! Now I'm not flying anymore, just hanging around the tactical headquarters.

I send you the warmest, deepest, most heartfelt wishes and kisses. I adore and love you, my Birthday Girl.

Me Too.

Always,

Your Don

2 May '68
Wednesday
9:30 pm

Hi Sweetie,

Been a long day of doing virtually nothing. I'm fine and well. All is quiet as the enemy has disappeared into the mountains. We can only find a few stragglers each day. A new experience for us and a quiet one.

Guess Fred arrived last night or today in Saigon and in a day or two he should arrive in Chu Lai.

Sent $500 to pay Diner's Club Hong Kong purchases. Still owe them $150, but I'll catch up soon.

Enclosed is a $100 money order and $179 Income Tax refund. I'm going to try to get a few days off once Fred arrives and get a few days' rest or maybe another R&R. I'm so darn tight and nervous since I was hurt on 14 April. It's not the cuts and scratches, it just gets to me. That was the third time and now I quit. Just quit charging around looking for trouble.

I still have $150 if you need more, I'll send you $100. Let me know, honey.

No mail from anyone in the last few days. Shit!

I count about 45 more days. Wunderbar! Hurry, hurry, hurry!

Dust off my love rug! Sprinkle on some perfume and douse yourself in powder and ahhhhhh! Home again.

Give a kiss to Stinky for me.

Love, need and want you.

Me too.

Always,

Your Don and Daddy

7 May '68
41 days!

Dearest Ruth,

Just a short note. All is well ... I am fine. Fred is here with me now. I met him in Chu Lai and have been getting him briefed, oriented and introduced all around to everyone. He is fine and in good spirits. Here he is

Hello my dear Sister,

I'm so glad and happy to be here with my "brother" and the wonderful officers and men of the First Cavalry and best unit in the Army. Don met me in Chu Lai and we stopped to see Jo Connoly on the way in here. Dianne and the children are fine. I hope all is well with you and Jacqueline. I know you can't wait to see your man! He will be home soon. Take care. Love and Kisses, Fred

The day after tomorrow I'm going to take an R&R to Sydney at the General's direction and come back to Chu Lai on 20 May and spend the remaining time there not doing much of anything and away from Combat.

I'm getting worn down to a frazzle and my nerves are pretty well shot by now. The long grind day after day has been hard.

Oh! I'm fine and just tired, baby, of all this crap of killing people and all.

Now that Fred is here he assumes all my duties and from now on I'm just not going to do anything but rest and try to unwind and not get involved in any operations.

Tomorrow I turn over my duties, bunker and everything to Fred. On the 20 May, when I return from R&R, they will give me a party and some medals at a ceremony. Then, like I said, I will be in Chu Lai until about 17 June.

Got your letter where we hit the 50 day mark and I smiled and I'm so happy you're so happy. Me too.

Kisses for Stinky.

I love and miss you so much. Me too.

Always,

Your Don and Daddy

8 May '68
Wednesday

Hi Sweetie!

I know this smiling picture will bring a smile to your face. Fred was happy to be here, and I am happy he has arrived.

In the morning my helicopter will take me to Da Nang and the day after I'll be on my way to Sydney for 5 days.

It will be a welcome change from the hell of February, March and April.

I'll try to buy one or two little souvenir gifts but I have only $150.

All is well. I'm fine.

I love, need, want and miss you.

Me too.

Always,

Your Don and Daddy
Happy Mother's Day, Big Momma

18 May '68
Saturday evening
10:40 pm

My Dearest Ruth,

Yeah! Your Big Daddy has been remiss in writing you the last few days, but all is well. I'm fine again and back in Vietnam.

I can't begin to describe the last few days, but I will try. Of course you have received the two short notes I wrote you from Sydney. But then, I got violently ill. First I had acute diarrhea, vomiting and wound up in Sydney General Hospital with intestinal flu for three days. God! I thought I had had it - even today. I still have not been able to eat without vomiting or running to the john. It's sickening! Then I accidently stuck a fork through my tongue had two stitches, lost a quart and a half of blood, got two shots and a whole lot of pain later, I still can't eat or chew. Jesus Christ! I'm a sad sack!

If I were ten years younger we would immigrate to Australia. It's a wonderful country. I was offered a job at $12,000 a year to start by the City Mayor as an industrial development advisor. With retirement pay, it would be over $23,000 a year. Guaranteed raises to $25,000 in 7 years. We shall talk about this later.

I was treated like a hero in Australia as the most combat decorated field grade officer to ever arrive there. I was on National television and all that stuff.

As you may have guessed just before I left for R&R, I was up to my neck in worry and, frankly darling, was a bit scared as I had never seen so much shit and horror as I have recently.

I told you I was wounded very lightly on 14 April but the truth is, I took a bullet through my left leg and right hand and I was hurting so bad, I couldn't walk. Oh yeah, you're bad Don. But as always, through the grace of God for me, and although I limp a little, I'm fine and dandy. Guess it hurt me mentally more than physically, but it began to scare the hell out of me.

Just before I went to Australia I went through the most severe emotional strain I've had in my Army career as the Generals offered me command of this squadron if I extended for six more months. For two days I fought all the inner battles in my head and heart and, OF COURSE, I decided to come home to you, my darling.

But the Army as good and great as it has been to me this year, made me all sorts of promises .... even having Fred as my X.O. and Rob Roller as my S-3. I listened to the Generals, but LORD, I love and need you, Ruth. Anyway, darling! I will tell you the whole story next month, but for sure ... I did the right thing. I've received more medals than any other Major in Vietnam, was wounded three times - each a lucky one - and made my mark as a hero. Now I'm ready for no more wars for a while. I need you, Jacqueline and rest.

Oh Ruth! Ruth! I just read seven days back mail from you and from your letters I just cry for you. My brave Big Momma. Poor Mutti! Me here, and you worrying yourself sick over her.

Darling, according to my most recent orders, I should depart Vietnam on or about 17 June and fly the US Embassy airplane to Frankfurt. I sent you my alert orders but the actual orders should arrive 10 days prior to my leaving.

Yes! Darling, I agree. We should go somewhere not so crowded and out of Fulda. You arrange it. Frankfurt, Bad Orb, just someplace for a few days. Then we can take a travel vacation for a week and then off to America, my darling.

I need you, the warmth of you, the love of you, the insides of you, the closeness and dearness of my good, sweet Big Momma. I'm so goddamn sick of here, of being shot at and hit at times and the bitterness of Vietnam. I've had it, sweetie. For nearly 10 months I've charged so hard to do well, to make a name for myself as an officer in combat. Now as I look back I shake violently at some of the things I've done for career and promotion. But like I always promised, it's for you, for us and I won. WON IT ALL. Thank God!

Yes! I miss you!

Yes! I love you as ever!

Yes! I want and need you!

Stay loose! I'll keep you posted on exact dates as soon as I know them. Right now it looks like....

17	June	Leave Vietnam
18	June	Arrive Frankfurt -
20	July	Leave Frankfurt
21	July	Back in America

We shall see. I want a vacation of at least a week to re-learn the insides of my loving wife. Garmisch, Frankfurt, I don't care. Just a bed ... and us!

All is well. I am back in the squadron again, still sick inside and I can't eat, but otherwise okay. Fred is sleeping just two feet away from me. He sends his love. Three days here and then I fly back to Chu Lai and spend the last 25 days there, rather than in combat. Yes! I'm happy. Tired, but happy. I probably have not answered all your questions from back mail but I shall do so tomorrow when I reread your letters.

I love, want, want, need, need and love the very heart and soul of you, my love. For tonight, me too.

Always,

Your Don and Daddy

21 May '68

Dearest Ruth,

Here I am finally in Chu Lai on the ocean. It's a very warm sunny morning and I'm sitting in my shorts in the sun outside my hooch. As I look out to sea, I can only think .... 26 more days and I'm on my way to you ... at last!!!!

In a couple of weeks it will be our 8th Anniversary. You have been such a brave girl, a loving wife, a wonderful mother and great for my career. For all the little and big things you do, I love you so. But most of all because you're you. Don't be sad, honey. Even though I'm not there, my heart is with you on our day.

We shall have a late anniversary party, sweetie, and I have a present for you ... as much and as many times as you like. How does that sound?

Happy Anniversary to my Ruth.

Love you.

Always,

Your Don

24 May '68
Friday Evening
1700 hours

Dearest Ruth,

I spent almost the entire day in the sun. I'm getting quite a good tan and have a real white bottom compared to the rest of me. Just like your tan last year in Texas.

I'm fine and the sun is really doing me good. Just horny for you ... I get so excited just thinking about you.

Fred has been quite sick from flying. He gets violently ill with air sickness, but that should pass in time. He has got to fly, so he has no choice. I haven't seen him at all this week since I'm now back in Chu Lai.

The squadron gave me a trophy Chinese rifle that we captured. It's a beautiful one and I shall carry it home with me.

With all my free time I'm writing efficiency reports and awards for my staff. Not much else to do. It won't take me more than five minutes to pack before I leave, so that's no problem.

Just whistle real loud, and I'll come home.

HOME! In about ~~IIII~~ ~~IIII~~ ~~IIII~~ ~~IIII~~ IIII

24 days! I can't believe it. It's just so great! Big Momma in bed again. Ooooo!

Give Jacqueline a big kiss from her Daddy.

Love to Mutti.

Love you.

Me too.

Always,

Your Don and Daddy

28 May '68
Tuesday Evening

Dearest Ruth,

All is fine! I'm well. Just eager to get the hell out of here. About 20 days and I'll be under way flying home to you and Stinky.

Sounds so good I can't believe it either. On 10th June the squadron is having a large formation, band, medals, goodbye gifts and party for me. It will be both a happy and sad day for me for the squadron has done so well here and I feel I have helped too.

Thank you, Stinky, for your letter with all the stars and letters.

The furniture you purchased sounds great. You're happy ... I'm happy.

I still eat only one meal a day because it comes up or out. No! Nobody bit my tongue! It's fine now and better to kiss you with. How's yours?

I thought you would like that picture of me and Fred! I laugh every time I see it too. You can see how happy I am that he arrived so I can leave.

I was up North all day yesterday at a Vietnamese medals ceremony. No, I didn't get one, but I had to go. I got one in March from the same battle.

Poor Fred. He still gets so sick flying in the helicopter. Hope he gets over this soon. He turns green, yellow and blue every time. He sends you his love and a kiss, too. And a hello to everyone.

General Koster, my boss, wrote a letter to Col. St. John asking him to give me the 1/14th Commander's job when I finish school. General Koster leaves here on 3 June and takes over West Point. If I don't get a command assignment in Europe he wants me to come to West Point.

Lt. General Mildren from Stuttgart comes to Vietnam in July but I'll wait until he's back in the United States to work for him.

How is Mutti? Love to her from her Donald Carl.

For this evening, I send my love. I need, want and love you. Me too. Always,

Your Don and Daddy
24 days to love rug time!

Sunday 2 June '68

Dearest Kittchen,

All is well! I'm fine! Don't you worry Big Momma. Aside from my patriotic and career hopes I love you and I'll be home soon. I've had enough of Vietnam and now want & need you, as I always have. Remember that everything I do is for us and on 20 June I'll be on my way to you in Frankfurt.

Ya! Hoo!
I need you!

In the morning around noon I fly to Saigon to get my passport and visas and should get back here for my goodbye party on the 7th June. Party is the 18th!

I'll write from Saigon. I love, need, want and miss you Sweetie. You too Stinky. I love you my Kittchen.

Ich auch

Amen,
Your Don & Daddy

6 June '68 Tuesday
Hotel Caravelle Saigon

Good Morning Sweetie,

I just awakened and it is 8:15 am Saigon time. Managed to beat the red tape and system and now have my passport and visas all set.

In a few minutes, Tom Streithouse of NBC News is coming over to interview me on my opinion and reactions to the shooting of Robert F. Kennedy. This is the man on the street-interview type and I've done this in combat with him several times before.

NBC gave me a room here and each evening they have bought my dinner and drinks. Most all of the TV news, ABC, CBS and NBC operate out of this hotel and I know them all from their visits to us in the field.

Saigon is like an ant hill with all the people scurrying about all day and then at 7 pm it is very still. One can see the burning parts of the city, rockets landing on Chalon. I watched for hours last night on the 10th floor roof and it is so sad to see.

Isn't that just enough to make one sick about Bobby Kennedy? If he survives this all, he will be a shoo-in to win the Democratic nomination now.

I will leave Saigon tomorrow providing I get a scheduled flight back to Chu Lai. I have a couple more things to check on today and will try to see Col. H if I can get transportation to where he is.

14 Big Days more and I'm home to my Big Momma. I'm so, so happy. You? Hmmmm!

Sitting here drinking coffee now. I guess in the last month this is only my second or third cup. Only my Ruth makes good coffee. Soon.

Money? While I think of it ... rather than sending you some now I will bring $600 in cash home with me. Hope you don't need anything until then. And before we leave Germany on 30 June, I'll draw some more money.

Well Ruth. In a few minutes Tom will be here and I must shave and clean up so that I look pretty on television back home.

For now my love. Soon, Big Momma. Soon! I need and love you. You, too, Jacqueline.

Me too.

Always,

Your Don and Daddy

11 June '68

My Dearest Ruth,

My heart is filled with such sadness and pride and anticipation and love for you. In a few short days I shall be home with you and Jacqueline and leave behind this place where I have spent almost a year.

My men had a wonderful party for me last evening and my heart is bursting with pride at their bravery and determination and I'm proud as hell of the job we have done together. We have achieved many great things and I feel we have all learned more than I even thought possible. I feel sadness for those who will be left here to carry on. I am finished ... I've done it all .... I am proud.

Now I will focus on the life that we will build for ourselves, for our Jacqueline. We will be together always now. My luck has held and now we can grow old together. Have a son together. Be a family together.

I will continue to give my all to the Army, but never again without you. We can now enjoy what I have given so many years to build.

First Armed Forces Staff College, then either West Point or my own squadron and then and then and then. We will achieve whatever we set out to do ... together.

I love you, my fellow soldier. It's our time next.

Give a kiss to my Stinky. Tell her Daddy is coming home.

I need, want, need, love and love you forever.

Me too.

Always,

Your Don and Daddy

OFFICE OF THE SUPERINTENDENT
UNITED STATES MILITARY ACADEMY
WEST POINT, NEW YORK 10996

MASP   19 March 1969

Lieutenant Colonel Donald C. Lundquist
Department of the Army
1st Battalion 64th Armor
3rd Infantry Division
APO New York 09031

Dear Don:

I'm indeed happy to hear you now command a tank battalion. I'm also pleased that I could recommend you for that most important position. You will find that commanding a battalion will be one of your most rewarding assignments.

Best of luck in the future.

Sincerely,

S. W. KOSTER
Major General, USA
Superintendent

THE REST OF THE STORY

On June 18 my father flew from Saigon to Calcutta and New Delhi, India to Rome and then to Frankfurt, Germany where my parents had a very emotional and long awaited reunion. After a couple of weeks of rest and rediscovery, we moved to Norfolk, Virginia where my father attended the Armed Forces Staff College. We lived right next door to Butch Saint and his family just as my father had planned. Those 6 months were a glorious time for my parents and they loved their life together. My father was invited to submit his name for consideration as the Military Attache to President Nixon but instead chose to command his own tank battalion in Kitzingen, Germany. We moved back to Germany in early March of 1969. I don't believe my parents could have been any happier. The "Year of the Tiger" was over, but they felt that this year would be the beginning of many new adventures and achievements together.

Then, a few weeks after their arrival, my grandmother finally succumbed to the cancer that she fought so bravely for so many years. She was 62. Six weeks later, on the morning of 17 April '69, my mother and I watched as my father took off in a helicopter for a two day training session with his tank battalion in Grafenwoer. We waved as his chopper flew higher and higher and finally disappeared into the sky. A few hours later, he was dead. While inspecting his troops, he suffered a massive heart attack and died within minutes. He was 38. I guess he'd say his luck had finally run out.

My mother, of course, was devastated. Her focus for a year had been on him surviving Vietnam. He had. The rest was supposed to be the easy part. That's what he had promised her. That's what she was counting on. You don't die. Not at 38.

My father's friends stepped in and helped my mother to make some decisions. His body was flown back to the United States and buried at Arlington National Cemetery among the soldiers he loved and respected so much.

After my father's death, we were forced to leave our military housing and lived for a short while with my aunts in Germany while my mother tried to regroup and plan the rest of our lives. That in and of itself was difficult, as she was only living one day at a time. Finally her decision was to move us back to the United States. We were both American citizens and she was certain my father would have wanted it that way. We settled in Northern Virginia just outside of Washington, D.C.

My mother decided initially not to work and just concentrate on raising me. The monthly pension we received from the military enabled us to live comfortably, yet modestly, and she worked hard to save her pennies. Enough, so that every summer we traveled to Germany for several months visiting relatives and exploring Europe. My childhood was happy and I never had want for anything. My parents' military friends, for the most part, ended up in Washington so I was surrounded by loving, caring and very generous people. My Godfather stepped up to his role and offered me encouragement, financial and emotional support and even the sex talk when I was a teen.

My beautiful, young and widowed mother decided to make me the sole focus of her life and she, above all, is the person I respect most in this world. She was filled with love and joy and full of hope. She did not become the suffering heroine. Her optimistic view of the world, despite everything that happened to her, is her single biggest gift to me. We basically grew up together and our relationship is a friendship above everything else.

Strangely, I have no recollection of my father. I had just turned five when he died and certainly should have memories of him. Just after his death, people would talk about what a great man my father was, and I would respond that I had no father. Visits to a child psychologist revealed that I was so angry with him for abandoning me that I just simply pretended he never existed. I can remember one day when I was six or seven, my mother dressed me up in my best dress and took me to visit his grave. I can vividly remember the lack of emotion I felt at seeing his name on the headstone. Over the years, we would take visiting friends and relatives to his gravesite and they would recite the most beautiful prayers and leave with tears in their eyes, obviously touched by being there. I felt nothing.

Then after reading his letters that summer of 1997 and then hearing his voice, I was overcome with a feeling of loss. Finally, he existed for me. I read his words to me. I listened to his Christmas carols, his birthday songs, stories of Easter and Thanksgiving. I heard the pain in his voice and also the pride. I came to know his views on race relations, the death of several prominent leaders and the politics of Vietnam. He was just doing his job as bravely and as conscientiously as possible. He loved his country, the Army, his job and, clearly, loved his wife, yet struggled to find the proper way to prioritize them. His dream was to one day become the Chairman of the Joint Chiefs of Staff. Many believe he would have accomplished that goal. Yet in the end, despite all his "charging" and heroism and patriotism, fate held for him another card. As unbelievable as he would have found it, he simply had a trumped heart.

Now it is three years later, the summer of 2000. I sit here in New Delhi, India and I finally compile his letters, I have once again rediscovered my father. Remarkably, I went from not knowing this man at all, to being able to finish his thoughts as I type his letters into the computer. I chuckle at his sense of humor. I blush at his words of longing to my mother. I know when he is not being honest with her about his injuries or his state of mind. I am filled with pride at his sense of duty and his allegiance to his fellow soldiers. I miss him and realize how different my life and my mother's would have been had he survived.

Yet, I am my father's daughter. I inherited his looks, his body type, his personality and his sense of humor. He was always the life of the party and I've been accused of that myself. His belief that "everything will work out" has become my mantra as well. I feel I've been blessed somehow and have always known that I would succeed at anything I set my mind to. Some people feel they are destined to do great things. I always have. For many years I thought fate was guiding me. Now I believe it is something, or should I say "someone" else.

Listening to his voice for the first time in three decades was initially a very disappointing experience. I had hoped that somewhere in the recesses of my mind I would remember it. As I listened, I found his voice not only unfamiliar but very strange. My father was born in the Bronx and raised in New Jersey but his accent was almost British. To me, he sounded just like Richard Burton. For almost an hour I listened without the slightest hint of recognition. Then, at the end of the tape he addressed me in German which was the only language I spoke at the time. A person's entire pitch and pattern of speech changes when they speak a different language. It was then that I remembered. What a strange and wonderful experience to hear a voice talk to you and say things that are so appropriate thirty years later.... "I'm sorry I can't be there for you" ... "take good care of your Mommy for me" ... "always remember that I love you even if it is from very far away!"

I know that many soldiers sent letters and tapes to their families during Vietnam. These correspondences obviously take on an entirely different importance if the person dies at an early age. Once my father returned from Vietnam both of my parents threatened to throw their respective boxes of letters away. "I will, if you will" was their common claim. But, thank God, neither ever did.

Finishing this book fills me once again with a sense of loss. Rereading and editing my father's letters made me feel close to him. Each day it was as though he was once again talking to me. I looked forward to his challenges, victories and even his sadness. The monsoon rains of India, where I now reside, were upon me as I worked on this book. Even sharing the same weather, albeit thirty monsoons later, gave me a sense of intimacy with him.

Perhaps because of my father's early demise, I am more conscious of the preciousness and uncertainty of life. In times of war, life hangs so preciously in the balance that one is forced to count their blessings at having survived the day. From a vast distance my father told my mother in no uncertain terms how much he loved and needed her almost every day. When they were together, they lived life voraciously. I often asked my mother why she didn't feel the need to marry again or be in a relationship with another man. Although my parents were only married for ten years before he died, she would always tell me that she had had it all. Quality not quantity is what counts in the end. I've let this be a lesson in my own life. It is one of the greatest gifts I possess.

I salute my father and I thank him for my spirit, my determination and his guidance. I do have a father. I know that now. And this book is for him.

Footnote:
Butch Saint when on to become a 4-Star General and retired just a few years ago and lives in Alexandria, Virginia. Fred Filbert survived his year in Vietnam, retired from the Army as a Colonel and lives in Colorado.

THE DEATH OF A LEADER

The death of Lt. Col. Carl Lundquist, CO, 1st Bn, 64th Armor, 3d Infantry Division, which occured April 17, 1969, at Grafenwöhr, is announced with deep regret.

Col. Lundquist assumed his position as CO, 1/64th Armor, on Feb. 8, 1969. At that time he expressed his anticipation of working with the battalion and ended his speech by saying, "Men, I accept command, and I feel now that I am home."

Under the able command of Col. Lundquist, the 1/64th Armor became the first Marne unit to lead the 1969 Combined Federal Campaign (CFC) with 100 per cent participation. The battalion later went on to become the top contributing unit of 1969, with many "We Piercers" donating $100 or more to CFC.

For the men of the 1/64th Armor, Easter couldn't be spent at home. Col. Lundquist figured that if this was the case, why not bring it to Grafenwöhr where the men were preparing for Tank Crew Qualification Course (TCQC).

Col. Lundquist arranged for special chartered busses and more than one hundred wives and children of 1/64th soldiers made the trip, had Easter dinner, and spent a pleasant afternoon at Graf.

Col Lundquist also brought his men the tenets of realistic training and combat readiness. Members of his command recently negotiated an 8000 meter land navigation course.

The armormen, who are accustomed to traveling in wheeled vehicles instead of walking, were given full instruction in all aspects of land navigation, map reading, and use of a compass. The troops found this program to be invaluable training and an asset to combat situations.

Armor tank gunnery incentives were begun under the command of Col. Lundquist. Before tank training, the battalion celebrated its Graf moveout with a party in their garrison city of Kitzingen.

Col. Lundquist came up with the idea for an Armor Queen of Tank Gunnery for boosting morale of the men training for Graf. He and Diana Rieder, Miss 42-A-GO-GO, awarded cash and prizes for the most unique mugs brought to the battalion celebration.

In addition to these training incentives, Col. Lundquist initiated an almost unbelievable group of prizes to be presented to each member of the high scoring tank crew at Grafenwöhr.

Col. Lundquist was born in Brooklyn, N.Y., November 21, 1930. He served in the Army National Guard from June 1947 through August 1948 and began active duty in September, 1948.

he was commissioned a second lieutenant, from Armor Officer Candidate School an March 7, 1956, and was promoted to lieutenant colonel on August 19, 1968.

Col. Lundquist was a graduate of Officer Basic and Career Courses, United States Army Armor School, Ft. Knox, Ky. He received a bachelor of arts from the University of Omaha in 1965 and later studied at the Armed Forces Staff College in Norfolk, Virginia.

Col. Lundquist served in the Korean War from April 1952 until June, 1953. In that conflict he participated in three major campaigns. After graduation from the Basic Officer Course, he served in Europe with the 14th Armored Cavalry Regiment. Upon his return to the U.S. he was an instructor at the U.S. Army Armor School for two years.

From February, 1965 to March, 1967 Col. Lundquist was assigned to Headquarters, 3d Inf Div as CMMI team chief in G-4 and as special project officer for tank gunnery in G-3.

He served with distinction as executive officer of the 1st Sqdn, 1st Cavalry Regiment, American Division in Vietnam.

Col. Lundquist has been awarded the Silver Star Medal, the Bronze Star Medal with "V" Device and two Oak Leaf Clusters, the Army Commendation Medal with Oak Leaf Cluster, the Air Medal with nine Oak Leaf Clusters and the Purple Heart with two Oak Leaf Clusters. In addition, he was awarded the Republic of South Vietnam Gallantry Cross with Gold Star and numerous service medals.

Col. Lundquist's career in the United States Army was marked by untiring zeal, outstanding merit and unswerving devotion to duty. His sudden death is a great loss to the U.S. Army and to the Marne Division.

Memorial services for Col. Lundquist werre held April 19, 1969 at the Larson Barracks Chapel in Kitzingen.

October 29th, 2009

Dear Dad,

I have known I was going to write to you for the past month or so, but just writing those two words, "Dear Dad" have already completely undone me. I have never written to you before because when you were alive, I was simply too young to write. I drew you pictures, which you said you treasured.

I am sitting in seat 24K on a United Airlines flight to Saigon. From there, I will travel to Danang and ultimately to Chu Lai where you were stationed. I know it sounds trite, but I am on a journey. A journey to find you and oddly, Vietnam is the only place where I believe I will feel close to you.

When you wrote those many hundreds of letters and recorded those tapes in your hooch over 40 years ago, your intention was to let your wife and daughter know you were okay. Never did you imagine that the only way I would ever get to know you would be through those words. So now, I will travel 10,000 miles to a country I have never seen in order to "find" you. I need to be where you were when you wrote them. I need to feel the driving rain of which you speak and that I can hear in the background of your tapes. I need to walk the soil you were protecting. I need to see the ocean that you patrolled by helicopter and dove in while trying to rescue injured men. I need to smell the air, and feel the heat, and see the faces of the people whom you fought to protect.

Your letters are beautiful in so many ways. Despite your hectic and emotional days, you took the time to write almost every day. I know it might sound silly, but your handwriting is beautiful. I can tell you were an artist - it is obvious in the curl and curve of each word. Your passion and love for your wife is stunning. I never knew mom as a wife and lover, but you convey that she was quite satisfying at both! I have read them enough times now that I no longer blush at your lustful musings. I love the way you respect and care for your soldiers. You were clearly an extraordinary leader and your military successes demonstrate that. Most of all, you are so articulate. I know you left high school to enlist in the army and serve in

Korea. I know you did not finish college until I was 2, yet you have a wonderful way with words.

I don't know exactly what I will find in Vietnam. For once, I am doing something without a plan, which is my usual M.O. Perhaps because you died, I felt I always had to be in control of every other aspect of my life. In high school, my friends always teased me, because my favorite words were, "Okay, here's the plan." I've continued on that track, planning events, trips and travel for hundreds of friends. But now, I go with only hotel reservations, and no real agenda.

I will let fate and serendipity guide my way. And, of course, you!

You have always been there. You have been my guardian angel, guiding me through the ridiculous and dangerous and spectacular adventures I have had. Somehow I felt no harm could befall me because you had your hand on my shoulder. Yet, almost every decision I have ever made was because you weren't there.

Your absence was present all the time.

Twelve years ago, I got to know you. I finally allowed myself to feel the pain of losing you just as I was about to give birth to my child. Once again, there is a milestone in my life, and I find the need to know you better. This time, however, I am angry with you. I need to tell you that somehow.

40 years ago you died. You left me, but more importantly, you left me all alone to deal with Ruth. Now, at almost 80, she has made the decision to leave DC and move to Colorado. Because you died, she is solely my responsibility. Because you died so young, you didn't have time to have other children with whom I could share the load. I am and have always been her everything. That is hard, hard work!

"Don't worry so much, Ruth," your letters say time and time again. Yet, that is all she does. Her worst fears came to fruition. They have never subsided.

I'm not sure why, but her move to Colorado shook her foundation and mine. She is as sad and vulnerable now as she was 40 years ago. I feel ill equipped to figure out how to make her happy?

So, I wing my way half way across the world. I will search for the strength you found while dealing with unbelievable horror and suffering. I will search for perspective, which you were able to find in the midst of utter chaos. I will search for peace in your world of war.

"Go sit on your mommy's lap, my little Jacqueline. Know that your daddy loves you and misses you and wants to be with you. Squeeze her tight and feel all the love that your daddy has for you. It will all be alright."

Always,

Your Jacqueline

October 31, 2009

Dear Dad,

I arrived in Vietnam last night after a flight from Colorado Springs, San Francisco and Hong Kong. I think I traveled for 34 hours. A far cry from the 2 weeks it took you to reach Vietnam from California in the summer of 1967. Saigon is now called Ho Chi Minh City. I just realized you never lived long enough to know what happened in the war you so bravely fought. On July 2, 1975 North Vietnam and South Vietnam merged to create the Socialist Republic of Vietnam.

I walked the streets today in an effort to find a trace of you. The Caravelle Hotel where you stayed when you came to Saigon still exists although now it is twice the size. The room you paid $22 for now goes for $280. My friend Indriena, who is making this journey with me and I went to the top floor and had a beer in the Saigon Saigon Bar. You and your friend, George, had drinks there almost 42 years ago to the day. I doubt it has changed much. Ceiling fans circulate the warm and humid tropical air and the cigar case still stands. Black and white photographs from a bygone era reflect the history of this once modern hotel.

I read a book about the war by an Australian journalist who said that you could see the war raging in the distance from the top of the hotel, as it was the tallest structure in town. There are now many high-rises and the Caravelle's ten stories no longer impress or impose.

I went to the Ben Thanh market where you purchased my red silk pajamas. I doubt that has changed much in the years. Hundreds of small stalls still sell every kind of imaginable crap! Shoes, fruit, laquerware, fans, beads and baubles, knock-off perfume—all amidst the smell of chickens and pigs fresh from the slaughter. Quite a place!

This morning I found a $5 dollar bill in my running shorts. A little girl Sam's age approached me in the market wanting to sell me hand carved and painted sandalwood fans for $3 each. I got three of them. She got my lucky $5 bill. Lana and I were both very, very happy.

The streets are wide and well paved and the roads are filled with thousands upon thousands of motor scooters. There are NO traffic lights, so if you want to cross the street, you simply start walking and hope beyond hope that the people stop, swerve or slow down. The process is amazing and somehow it works. At least, so far.

Tailors are still the rage and every other store sells fabrics and designs that will fashion you an outfit in 3 days. The most amazing sight to me was that every 50 yards or so there is a little kiosk that sells remnants of the war. Glass cases are filled with watches and lighters and talisman from soldiers that died. Silver lighters, just like the one Mom gave you, that have quotes from friends and lovers inscribed on them. The war ended 34 years ago but you can still buy a lighter that says "If I die in Vietnam, bury me upside down so that the army can kiss my ass."

There are Timex and Rolex and other watches that must have been ripped off the bodies of dead soldiers. So very, very sad.

We walked along the Saigon River and watched children catching crabs with their fishing nets. We immediately booked a table at Maxim's and pre-ordered the biggest crabs they have for dinner! Then we crossed the Tao Dan Park to head to the War Museum. Trees hundreds of feet tall with lush canopies right in the middle of the city. I'm sure Saigon looked more like that when you were here.

Without a doubt, I was ill-prepared for the war museum. The front lawn is dotted with tanks, helicopters, fighter planes, missiles and other US military arsenal. Inside, the open atrium 2-story building simply has photographs of the war with captions underneath. The story they tell, however, is very different from the one you write about. The horror of the photographs is mind-numbing. I literally walked through the building with my mouth agape and found it difficult to breathe. One photograph was of a soldier from your division holding up half a person's body on a stick with the caption "Soldiers from the 1st Cavalry division torturing an innocent peasant in the Hinh Khe district."

Another wall showed horrific photographs of women and children malformed from the effects of Agent Orange. Wall after wall of dead children, innocent victims of the horror rained down upon by the United States of America. "American soldiers execute innocent patriots." The propaganda is chilling.

I kept thinking of your words about your soldiers. You talk about their bravery. You talk about their fortitude. You talk about how they risked and gave their lives to fight for the freedom of a people 10,000 miles away. In the end, however, thousands of people walk through that museum every day and hear a very different story. And just outside, I can buy Captain Sheldon's dogtags for $8. Eisch!

I climbed into the helicopter outside. So many of your letters talk about the untold hours you spent patrolling the Vietnamese countryside looking for VC, delivering supplies and medivacing wounded soldiers. I felt closest to you there. Often the only "air" you got was while you were flying. I stared down the gun barrel of the automatic weapon that is bolted to the floor of the chopper and remembered your words.

"Today while I was flying the ABC news crew into the countryside, I spotted 10 Vietcong running across the field. I shot 6 of them. Then we set the chopper down and evacuated four of the wounded to our VC hospital. I'm being put in for a medal, while just serving as a passenger, so to speak."

Tomorrow we head to the Chu Chi tunnel. I'm looking forward to seeing the Vietnamese countryside. Cities are cities. I could really be anywhere in Asia. But first, we shall head to Maxim's for dinner. Crabs await!

Always,

Your Jacqueline

November 1, 2009

Dear Dad,

Today we left the hustle and bustle of the city and hired a car and driver to take us 70 kilometers outside of town to Cu Chi. While there, we explored the tunnels the villagers built at the start of the war with the French in 1948 and continued on for the next 30 years. The countryside is simply beautiful and I doubt has changed much since the last century. The emerald green pastures are spotted with brown cows and large grey water buffalo. The roads are well paved and as always, we were surrounded by motor scooters on all sides.

At Cu Chi, we were met by a guide who walked us into the jungle. The forests were thick and lush with hanging vines adorned with barbed wiry looking thorns. Given the history of the region, it seemed somehow fitting that even the trees were inhospitable.

We were led to a covered pavilion where we watched a 20-minute documentary from 1967. The grainy black and white footage paid tribute to the men and women freedom fighters who fought against the policies of the "crazy gang of devils in Washington." These "American killing heroes" included girls as young as 14 who learned to launch grenades and fire guns and rocket launchers at the Americans.

Cu Chi was the center of a 250 kilometers series of underground tunnels and rooms that connected the villages surrounding Saigon and allowed the Vietcong to stealthily destroy tanks and kill many thousands of American soldiers. Some 16,000 Vietcong lived their lives underground. 12,000 of them died.

Our guide, a lovely young man of 30, informed us that his grandfather and grandmother both were fighters. His grandfather died but his grandmother survived because she knew how to "walk without making a step, talk without making a sound and cook without making any smoke."

The tunnels are a remarkable feat of engineering. Using only a small shovel and a basket of bamboo to carry out the excavated dirt, the peasants created an underground world. The tunnels have three levels, 3 meters to 30 meters below the ground. There are kitchens, dining halls and command centers, bedrooms and hospital rooms. The rooms are connected by long tunnels no taller than 36 inches. We crouched down and made our way through them.

The experience was incredibly unnerving and quite literally took our breath away. The air was thick with humidity. Bats flew by our heads as only a small flashlight led our way through the intricate labyrinth. Our hearts were beating out of our chests when we finally emerged up a flight of dirt stairs back to the earth's surface.

Air holes disguised as termite hills allowed the VC and us to breath underground. Water wells were dug to provide drinking water and the smoke from the kitchens was redirected to a series of vents so that a single plume of smoke could not be spotted by the helicopters that flew overhead constantly in search of these illusive tunnels. The surrounding jungle is dotted by craters created by the bombs from B-52's that were dropped in a vain attempt to destroy the underground outpost.

I tunneled with our guide the entire length. Feeling uncomfortable was something I wanted to experience. At the end of the tour we went back down to the largest of the kitchens and drank tea and ate a basket of steamed cassava. We were then joined by a large group of Vietnamese tourists. Only one young 10-year old boy spoke English. His father encouraged him to talk to us. His English was superb and father beamed with pride that he was communicating with us.

"American killing heroes" children are serving me tea. The daughter of a "crazy devil soldier" is being shown wonderful hospitality. It's all very confusing. I asked our guide how he felt about this dichotomy. He said that in the 7 years he has been working there he has met many Americans. Whereas before he may have been angry, he now understands that the actions and directions of a person's government don't always reflect the will of the man. Amen to that.

We then went to visit a beautiful temple dedicated to Ho Chi Minh and the soldiers that died for the "freedom" struggle. I lit incense for our dead soldiers. I lit incense for theirs.

On the road back, we passed by a recent motor scooter accident. Two young boys lay dead in the street. Blood trickled from their noses and mouth. Our driver clicked his tongue and just drove on. The scene was surreal - and so hauntingly familiar.

I am sitting on the 18th floor of the hotel watching the sun set over Saigon. The sky is on fire! This time however, it is just the perfect combination of clouds and pollution.

Tomorrow we fly to Danang. I will be a step closer to you even still.

Always,

Your Jacqueline

PS - As Indy and I walked through the jungle, we passed a man. He was wearing a red t-shirt. The shirt had a scene on it that looked vaguely familiar and the words "Garden of the Gods." I grabbed him and told him I was from Colorado Springs. "Most beautiful place on earth," he responded. I asked him where he lived. He said "Jakarta." Indy flipped. What are the chances?

PPS - Indy and I are going to have dinner at Brad and Angelina's favorite restaurant. My, how times have changed!

November 2, 2009

Dear Dad,

I am here.

Today we arrived in Danang. As the airbus landed on the same strip of runway you used, the plane shimmied and shook on the descent. The driving rains and whipping winds tossed us all about. *"It rained like hell. Not straight down, but sideways."* The gusts of wind roared up from the ocean and sounded like low flying planes above my head. Perfect weather!

Our driver took us to China Beach. The ocean was angry with waves and sand and water spilled over the road making it a difficult drive. I saw the military base where you unloaded your ammunition and equipment before heading down to Chu Lai. The compound still stands and is now used as headquarters for an oil company. The miles of strand adjacent to the beach are all under construction. Chinese investors are building grand beachside resorts. Acres upon acres of planned houses, condominium time-shares, hotels, pools and tennis courts.

We drove down the coast to Hoi An. Our driver told us his father worked as a driver for the Americans during the war.

"That is Marble Mountain," he pointed to a hill in the distance.

"Americans shoot Vietcong up there. Hee Hee. Bang Bang."

I couldn't be happier. It is simple here. Not much has changed in 42 years. I am seeing the same things you saw. Perhaps even meeting the children of people you interacted with. I have booked a guide to take us to Chu Lai tomorrow. Armed with your maps and drawings and photographs and descriptions, I will find you.

You are here.

Always,

Your Jacqueline

November 3, 2009

Dear Dad,

"A long day just about gone!" Thus began your letter of November 3, 1967. I can say the same.

Today I walked in your footsteps.

I stood in the same spots. I saw the same sights. I met the same people.

This morning we made our way from Hoi An to Chu Lai with Minh, the driver who picked us up from the airport yesterday. Today was his day off, but like his father before him, he wanted to be the driver for this American's mission. His friend, Anh, a travel guide, accompanied us. Respecting one's ancestors is held in high regard here and both men were sleuth-like in their determination to help me find you. And honored, too.

They studied the maps you drew. They looked at the photos for clues.

I had your wallet in my purse. And the photos that you had in it. I brought your purple heart. Even though you didn't die here, I feel your time here weakened yours.

I had your letters. And your tapes. I had as much of you with me as there is left.

"Chu lai is a tremendous US Marine jet fighter base which bombs North Vietnam 24 hours a day. We and many other units are responsible for protecting the airbase from the Vietcong."

Much like this day 42 years ago, the monsoon clouds hung low in the sky giving the landscape of Chu Lai an eerie otherworldly feel. We drove past the airbase and to the beach on which you landed at 2:30pm on August 29, 1967. The winds were strong and mountains of waves pounded the beach. The grey of the sky and the gray of the ocean were indiscernible. The rough ocean unnerved me. Gusts of sand lashed against my legs. Unlike most beaches which give me a sense of peace, this place simply scared me. I stood there longer than I wanted to trying to understand the fear you must have felt.

I walked back to the car and Minh and Anh were engaged in conversation with a local woman. She had worked for the Americans. She spoke perfect English. I showed her pictures of you, of mom and of us. She knew exactly where you had been. Just a mile or so up the road.

"We all call where we are at troop headquarters 'Fat City.' It started as a joke and my energetic and humor minded Captains had a sign made which is an absolute riot. We have so much fun with the name. Everyone who comes in here laughs. That's good, for we need to laugh and smile every once in a while. Enclosed are a couple of shots taken this afternoon."

We drove up Highway 1. The wind whipped drifts of sand up onto the highway 12-18 inches deep in spots. Our car carved through the drifts just like snow. Sand dunes and ocean framed the left side of our vista and a tall wall the right. Minh stopped the car at a spot where the wall had crumbled down. It was, remarkably, the site of your sign!

Welcome to Fat City
Major Donald C. Lundquist, Mayor
-Air Conditioned Club and Guest Rooms
-Gambling Casino
-Swimming Pool
-Nightly Floor Shows
-Excellent Dining
-Air Shows
-Shooting Gallery
Blackhawk Support

The sign, of course, was long gone, but the views were identical. I held the photo. I beheld the view.

It started to rain. Anh ran out to me with an umbrella. Indrit ran over to take a photo wearing our hotel's complimentary rain poncho. She looked like a giant condom ambling toward me. I laughed. I cried.

You were here! Now I was.

We drove to the airbase which is now Chu Lai International Airport. It was closed because of the weather. We found the exact spot on the hillside where you first set up camp. The concrete pads for the helicopter landing site were cracked and spotted with weeds, but they were still there.

Indrit read your letter of November 3 (my favorite letter) out loud. We listened to your voice.

We drove into town and I invited Minh and Anh for lunch. We found a little spot on the road. Anh smiled and took me by the hand to show me something. Above the door lentil was a date stamp. 1967. Rose cooked for us as her mother had done for the Americans that dined there. Her husband did their laundry. "Yes," said Rose's husband, "I did washing for Lundquist. Jimmy Lundquist. Right? Never forget a name."

That would have been too much, anyway.

The Vietnamese guidebook indicates that "One of the great benefits to humankind brought about by the policy of Doi Moi (the free market) is a plentitude of beer. It is as common as water and more worthy. You will never be more than a few minutes from beer."

I ordered a 333 and we toasted you.

"Okay, now we go?" asked Anh.

Okay. Now we go.

Driving back we passed through villages familiar to me from your letters. Places where you *"accomplished the impossible combat mission, liberated a village after 11 years of VC control,"* and won medal after medal for *"gallantry in action against a hostile force."* They are now all peaceful hamlets where people go about the business of life.

I suppose the only thing that is guaranteed in life is that things change. War. Peace. Life. Death. Youth. Age.

Last night Indrit took me to the beach. We sat in the darkness. "Tell him you forgive him for dying. Say it. Out loud. Come on. You can do it. You must do it."

"Daddy. I forgive you for dying."

"Come here little Stinky. Do you miss your Daddy? Do you love your Daddy? He misses you sooooo much. And he loves you sooooo much. Soon I'll be home and we'll have lots of fun. Won't that be nice? Now go to bed and say your prayers and have nice dreams."

Always,

Your Jacqueline

November 4, 2009

Dear Dad,

Today the sun finally came out. The irony is not lost on me.

I sat by the pool reading the Lonely Planet Guide For People Who Like to Eat, Drink and Travel (did they write that just for me?). It quoted a Tet Proverb that resonated with me. "Trees have roots; water has a source, and when drinking from the spring, one must remember the source."

Tet is a three-day festival in January or February designed to pay homage to generations of deceased family members. The word Tet comes from the Vietnamese word Tiet which literally means "the knotty area between two sections of a stalk of bamboo." This conjoining represents the connection that holds us all together.

On the first day of Tet, families whisper the names of the spirits they wish to invoke. On the second, families visit the places their ancestor lived. On the final day, people visit their astrologers and find out their fortune for the New Year. "And on the evening of the third day, the ancestors depart, with smoke from burning votives assisting them in their flight."

Coincidentally, a friend sent me my horoscope today. It said:

"Do you feel like celebrating? You might, and if you do, you should! Saturn, the planet that tests us and presents challenges, has opposed your Sun, but on October 29, Saturn finally moved out of Virgo, the place that has been so difficult for you. The peacefulness you will soon feel will be sweet indeed. Dear Pisces, you have journeyed through dark and frozen tundra, but now, as November begins, you will start to see the first pink rays of dawn. Soon you will feel your old energy and optimism return. You won't feel as isolated as you may have felt in the past, and problems that weighed heavily on your shoulders will begin to lift.

As the month begins, it appears you will bring a writing project to fruition. Some sort of communications project is reaching an end point - and it will make you proud. This full moon is in conversation with Pluto, so you will find you feel pride about what you accomplished and a friend may figure very prominently in your success - he or she may help you in a very positive way."

I fashioned a boat of sorts and stuffed it with a photo of you and me. I drew you a picture of *"those pretty stars and those funny stick people with their arms and legs coming out of their heads."* I also included a US and Vietnamese flag. Then I set it asail in the South China Sea. I had my own Tet with you. It was just a couple of months early. Or, perhaps it was years late.

Always,

Your Jacqueline

November 7, 2009
Kuala Lumpur Airport

Dear Dad,

This may be the last time I write to you.

I have left Vietnam and am transiting through Malaysia on my way to my beloved India. There I will spend the next several weeks traveling through a country and with a people I love.

I am bone tired. Every bit of me is exhausted.

We spent the last days of our journey in the quaint little fishing village of Hoi An. My "mission" being "accomplished" we decided to be tourists and play. We had dresses tailored from beautiful brocade silk. We wandered the narrow alleys and perused the shops. We ate delicious meals, and had massages, and took in the intense South Asian sun.

We frequented the clubs and bars where we met and chatted with droves of young 20-somethings from all over the world backpacking their way through South Asia. A dashing young man from Canada named Jack who just finished college and was trying to find his path far from the shadow of his famous journalist father. Erica and Allen from England who will spend the year "seeing where the tides take them" stopping along the way and working when their money runs out. Six Danish beauties who just wanted to have world experiences before they finished college and settled down.

I thought of the thousands upon thousands of 20-somethings that were here with you. So many of them gave their lives. So many did not have a choice. To think that this would someday be a place where people came to get lost intentionally!

In a single word, I found Vietnam "unimposing." It is so unlike India, which assaults ones senses at every turn. It is efficient and well run. Things move on time and in an organized way. The people are polite and unobstrusive. They are neither tall nor short, attractive nor ugly, stylish nor garish. I saw no fabulous wealth nor abject poverty. It is absolutely safe and we never felt threatened in any way. No one drives too fast, eats to excess, or shows great emotion of any kind. It is absolutely unremarkable in every way.

Yet, this very same place unleashed the fiercest of emotions and actions from you.

"I'm so god-damned sick of here, of being shot at and hit at times and the bitterness of Vietnam. I've had it, sweetie. For nearly 10 months I've charged so hard to do well, to make a name for myself as and officer in combat and now I look back and I shake violently at some of the things I've done for career and promotion. But like I always promised, it's for you, for us and I won. WON IT ALL. Thank God!

The pressure on a man here is something terrific and to keep it up seven days a week, month in and month out, is greater than I expected and have ever faced in my life. It has scared me many, many times but I thank my stars I won these battles with myself and came out of them the right way each time."

Sometimes the actions and directions of one's government do not represent the will of the man.

We stayed up until the dawn on our last night. We danced on the beach with abandon and complete release. We laughed too hard and drank too much and celebrated freedom.

I've been sharing these letters with a handful of close friends. One friend sent me an email and said that she thought that my trip to Chu Lai may have been one of the "biggest" days of my life. I've thought about that so many times. I've always thought of "big" days as days of joy. Your wedding day. Your due date. The start of a vacation or a new job. But she was right.

It was scary. It was ominous. It was emotional. It was trailblazing. It was necessary. It was BIG!

"I love you both, my Blondies! Be good to each other. Daddy is fine. He just misses his baby and Big Momma. I shall be so happy to get out of here, home to you both, a house, a home, a warm bed full of love, full of you.

You will have to bear with me for a while for as much as I miss the comfort of a good night's sleep, I know it will take time for this Big Daddy of yours to adjust again to warmth and peace at night."

I miss you, Big Daddy. I shall take care of your beloved Ruth, and she of me, as we have always done.

Be at peace. I am.

Always,

Your Jacqueline

The President of the United States of America, authorized by Act of Congress, July 20, 1942, has awarded the Legion of Merit posthumously to

LIEUTENANT COLONEL DONALD C. LUNDQUIST, U S A

for exceptionally meritorious conduct in the performance of outstanding services:

Lieutenant Colonel DONALD C. LUNDQUIST, Armor, distinguished himself by outstanding performance of duty in a position of great importance as Commanding Officer, 1st Battalion, 64th Armor, 3d Infantry Division, United States Army, Europe, from February 1969 to April 1969. Through superior leadership, persistence, and professional skills, Lieutenant Colonel LUNDQUIST developed his battalion into a closely knit, highly motivated and combat ready organization which continually excelled in all fields of endeavor. His dynamic leadership enabled him to mold his men into a highly efficient team, resulting in record scores during the 1969 Tank Crew Qualification Course and during command inspections. He unceasingly gave of his own energies to inspire confidence and instill esprit de corps within his unit. His knowledge, devotion to duty and ability to grasp the implications of new problems won for him the respect and admiration of all with whom he served. Lieutenant Colonel LUNDQUIST's commendable achievements and outstanding performance of duty have been in keeping with the highest traditions of the military service and reflect distinct credit on him and the United States Army.